The Great Game Book

The Great Game Book

A superb collection of game recipes
from the finest restaurants in Great Britain
and Ireland

Absolute Press

Published by Absolute Press (publishers)
14 Widcombe Crescent, Widcombe Hill, Bath, Avon.
Tel: (0225) 316013

First published November 1986

© Absolute Press

Editor **Paula Borton**

Cover printed by
Stopside Ltd, Windsor Bridge Road, Bath.

Phototypeset by
Sulis Typesetting, 2 Gay Street, Bath.

Printed by
WBC Print, Barton Manor, St. Philips, Bristol.

Bound by WBC Bookbinders, Maesteg.

Contents

Introduction

The ever increasing use of chemicals and food additives in modern farming and food production has meant that many enthusiastic cooks have turned their attentions away from mass produced butchery in favour of more natural techniques of farming and cultivation. Interest has naturally focused upon game produce, arguably the most pure and fine flavoured meat available. Game cookery has a long and distinguished history in Britain, yet over the last century the quantity and variety of game available to domestic cooks has sadly diminished. But things are beginning to change for the better. Enthusiastic game wholesalers and suppliers are spreading not only the word but also the produce far and wide. A general re-education, of both retailer and consumer, is taking place. Today a number of the larger supermarket chains have been persuaded to experiment with game – to great success. Family butchers are now responding to the renewed demand and are actively searching out good and reliable sources of supply.

And in the kitchens of the great restaurants game cookery is finding new favour. Such is the variety and versatility of game that a whole cuisine can be built around it. The editors of The Great Game Book approached the leading chefs known to be enthusiastic about game and asked them to contribute their favourite recipes. The result is a really superb collection of the classical and the new, the simple and the sophisticated. A collection of recipes which it is hoped will help in the campaign to re-establish the delightful habit of eating and enjoying game.

Grouse

August 12th – December 12th

Terrine of Grouse

Pool Court, Pool-in-Wharfedale
Chef Melvin Jordan

Serves 8–10

1 brace grouse
8 rashers mild smoked bacon
8 oz. (225g.) pork, finely
   chopped
6 fl. oz. (175ml.) chicken or
   grouse stock
1 clove garlic, crushed
1 sprig thyme
salt and freshly ground pepper
2–3 fl. oz. (50–75ml.) brandy

Remove the breasts from the grouse and cut into strips ¼"
(0.5cm.) thick. Take as much flesh off the rest of the grouse
as possible. Marinate the strips of meat in the brandy for
about one hour.

Line a 12" (30.5cm.) terrine mould with the bacon. Leave
the breasts to one side, and place the remaining meat and
livers from the birds, pork, garlic and thyme in a blender.
Chop coarsely, season and place the mixture into the
terrine with reserved strips of grouse in the centre. Pour
over stock and brandy and cover with a buttered lid.

Place the terrine in a tray and surround with 2" (5cm.) of hot
water. Cook in the oven for 1–1¼ hours at 350F/180C/Gas
4. Remove the lid and place weights on top to press until
quite cold. Place in the fridge to set. To turn out, run hot
water over sides and bottom of mould and shake onto a
board or plate. Return to refrigerator before slicing.

Roast Young Scottish Grouse

The Peat Inn, Peat Inn
Chef/proprietor David Wilson

Serves 6

6 young grouse, prepared with
   livers reserved
6 rashers of streaky bacon
5 fl. oz. (150ml.) of good game
   stock
5 fl. oz. (150ml.) red wine
6 croutons about 1¼" (3cm.) in
   diameter
4 oz. (125g.) unsalted butter
dash sherry vinegar
brandy and port, small
   quantities to finish sauce
salt and pepper

The young grouse is such a delicate, tender and flavoursome bird that I recommend the most simple treatment.

Place the birds in a roasting tin and cover breasts with bacon. Ensure the birds are not packed too tightly in the roasting tin or they will not cook evenly. Pour a little game stock and red wine just to cover the bottom of the tin. Place the tins on the middle shelf and in a preheated oven at 450F/230C/Gas 8 and cook for about 20 minutes. Check the birds by feeling the breasts – they should just respond when pressed, feeling neither too firm or too soft. The birds will then be cooked but still pink.

Remove the birds from the oven and allow to rest for a few minutes, in a cool oven or warming drawer. Reserve the bacon. Pour off all the liquid in the roasting tin into a saucepan.

Remove the tray from the warming drawer, carve the breasts keeping one piece and remove skin. Chop off the legs and remove skin. Place the breasts and legs back in the tray and keep warm.

Fry the croutons in a little butter, keep warm. Lightly fry the livers and place on top of the warmed croutons.

To make the sauce, chop up one carcass and place in a saucepan with the reserved cooking juices. Add the remainder of the game stock and bring to the boil. Simmer for 5 minutes. Pass the sauce through a sieve pressing through all the juices. Bring back to the boil and reduce to the required consistency. To finish add pieces of butter and whisk into the sauce. Finally, add a drop of vinegar and a little brandy and port. Check seasoning.

To serve, place the breasts side by side on a plate. Position the legs left and right at the top of the plate. Place the croutons in the centre. Roll the reserved bacon around your finger and place in front of the crouton between the breasts. Pour sauce around and not over. Serve immediately.

Roast Grouse 'my favourite game dish'

Fox & Goose, Fressingfield
Chef A. P. Clarke

Serves 4

4 fresh grouse
12 pieces of fat streaky bacon
4 pieces of white bread
salt and pepper

This is the simplest and best game dish there is. The grouse is the only game bird that is naturally gamey and thus needs no hanging. This is due to the fact that the grouse season starts in mid-August which is usually a warm and humid month and therefore brings the bird on that much quicker. Do try and buy fresh grouse that has been gutted but that has had the heart and liver left in.

Bard and lard the grouse and then place on pieces of bread. Pre-heat the oven to 425F/220C/Gas 7 and cook the grouse for 20 minutes – they must be pink. Remove the barding and allow them to rest in the bottom of a cool oven for 15 minutes. Serve these wonderful birds with bread sauce and a rich gravy. A meal to be remembered!

Grouse Grand Veneur

La Ciboulette, Cheltenham
Chef/proprietor Kevin Jenkins

1–2 well hung grouse
½ bottle red wine
2 carrots, chopped
1 small onion, chopped
½ bay leaf
sprig of thyme and rosemary
1 clove garlic, chopped
6 black peppercorns
½ pint (275ml.) game or veal
   stock
1 tablespoon redcurrant jelly
1 tablespoon red wine vinegar
½ baked apple, to garnish
stem of fresh redcurrants, to
   garnish

Marinate the grouse in wine and vegetables for 24 hours.

Drain off the vegetables. Roast the grouse in a hot oven, keeping the meat pink.

Fry the vegetables in oil and butter until golden brown. Deglaze the pan with vinegar, reduce and then add the wine and reduce again by ¾. Add the stock and redcurrant jelly and boil until the sauce becomes syrupy. To finish, whisk in a few knobs of butter.

Coat the grouse with the sauce and garnish with half a baked apple and a stem of fresh redcurrants.

Roast Grouse with Port and Madeira

Sharrow Bay, Ullswater
Chefs Juan Martin and Colin Akrigg

Serves 4

4 grouse, prepared (retain livers)
1 small onion, chopped
2 sticks celery, chopped
1 eating apple, chopped
2 tablespoons port
2 tablespoons Madeira
½ pint (275ml.) grouse or game stock
4 oz. (125g.) butter
1 tablespoon vegetable oil
4 heart shaped croutons
4 slices bacon

In a frying pan sweat the chopped celery, apple and onion. Place on a roasting tray.

Seal the grouse in a hot pan of oil. Brush with butter and place on the roasting tray. Put slices of bacon over the birds and cook in a hot oven for 25 minutes or until cooked to preference.

Deglaze the roasting tray with the port and Madeira. Add the stock and reduce to thicken to desired consistency, retaining the celery, apple and onion.

Make a pâté by cleaning and preparing the grouse livers. Seal them in a hot pan. Liquidise and add 1 oz. (25g.) butter. Season with a splash of brandy, salt and pepper.

To serve, place the liver pâté on the cooked croutons. Take the grouse off the bone and arrange the croutons with a little of the sauce, celery, apple and onion round. You could also serve the grouse accompanied with bread sauce, allumette potatoes, grilled bacon and fried breadcrumbs as an alternative.

Roast Grouse with Spiced Damsons

The Wife of Bath, Wye
Chef/proprietor Bob Johnson

1 young grouse per person
piece of toast per bird
liver paté
red wine
butter
salt and black pepper

For the spiced damsons:

2 lb. (900g.) damsons
3 cups red wine
1½ cups red wine vinegar
10 cloves
2 cinnamon sticks
1 teaspoon ground ginger
8 oz. (225g.) brown sugar

Put all the ingredients for the spiced damsons, except for the damsons, into a pan, bring to the boil and cook for 15 minutes. Pour into a preserving jar and add the damsons. Leave for at least 2 days, preferably longer.

To cook, melt some butter in a heavy frying pan, season the birds and press breast side down, browning slightly. Turn the birds onto other breast and cook for about 7 minutes in a very hot oven. After 7 minutes turn the birds again and cook for a further 7 minutes. The birds should be just pink.

Remove the birds onto a piece of toast covered with liver paté. Return the pan to the heat, add a dash of red wine to the pan juices and swish around. Serve the sauce separately with grouse and spiced damsons. A few game chips and runner beans are an ideal addition to this dish.

Grouse Bohemian Style

The Old Manor House, Romsey
Chef/proprietor Mauro Bregoli

Serves 2 or 4 depending on whether you serve a whole or half grouse

2 young grouse
2 beaten eggs
4 cups brown breadcrumbs
1 tablespoon crushed coriander
   seeds
salt and pepper
1 lemon
3 oz. (75g.) butter

Split the grouse down the backbone, press gently and season well.

Mix the breadcrumbs and crushed coriander together. Pass the grouse in beaten egg, then the breadcrumbs and coriander mixture, making sure that they are well coated.

Fry very, very gently in the melted butter for 20 minutes. Sprinkle the now golden birds with fresh lemon juice and serve immediately.

Casseroled Grouse with Pears

The Old Manor House, Romsey
Chef/proprietor Mauro Bregoli

2 grouse (they could be old)
18 oz. (500g.) pears, peeled
  and cored
½ pint (275ml.) single cream
1 oz. (25g.) butter
6 rashers streaky bacon
salt and pepper
1 measure eau de vie de Poire
  Williams

Cover each breast of grouse with 3 rashers of bacon and truss. Melt half the butter in a heavy casserole, add the grouse and sauté until golden. Reduce the heat, add the rest of the butter, the pears and salt and pepper to taste. Cook for 15 minutes stirring occasionally so that the pears are brown. Add the cream, cover and cook for a further 30 minutes.

5 minutes before the end of the cooking time, remove the bacon so that the breasts become browned. Just before serving add the eau de vie – bring to the table in the casserole.

Grouse Crumble

Paul's, Folkestone
Chef/proprietor Paul Hagger

6 grouse (casserole or old
   grouse are best and much
   cheaper)
2 large onions
2 large carrots
4 oz. (125g.) streaky bacon
2½ oz. (65g.) butter
5 fl. oz. (150ml.) red wine
1 oz. (25g.) bramble jelly
   (redcurrant jelly or even
   brown sugar will do)
freshly ground black pepper
   corns
a few fresh herbs, according to
   preference
1½ oz. (40g.) mild chilli relish
chicken stock
seasoning
a little cornflour mixed with
   water to thicken gravy

Give the grouse to a kitchen help to pluck, gut, rinse and pat dry.

Place a thick bottomed pot onto a fierce heat, large enough to take all the ingredients and add the butter. When brown, fry the grouse till golden, remove and set aside. Fry the bacon – when golden remove leaving the fat. Fry the sliced onions till golden then add the carrots and celery – fry a little longer.

Place everything into the pot and just cover with a really good chicken stock (prepared by your kitchen help over the last 3 days). Cover with a lid and slowly cook, stirring occasionally. This is best done in a moderate oven. Cook until it is easy to pull a leg off one of the bigger birds – if you can't find any legs perhaps you have slightly over done the last stage!

Remove the grouse and allow to cool.

Thicken the boiling casserole sauce with the cornflour mix, keep the liquid boiling and stir all the time. Thicken till the consistency of double cream, runny not whipped. Allow to cool.

For the crumble topping:

4 oz. (125g.) wholemeal flour
4 oz. (125g.) butter
3 oz. (75g.) grated cheese

Remove the meat from the cool grouse, keeping the breast meat as large as possible. Add to the thickened casserole sauce.

You are now ready to portion the casserole into individual ovenproof dishes or one large ovenproof casserole. If you wish this dish will now: a) freeze b) keep in the fridge for up to 3 days c) sprinkle with crumble mix and cook immediately.

To serve, sprinkle on cheese crumble topping and bake in a moderately hot oven till the topping goes golden and the casserole is bubbling around the eges. If, through no fault of your own, your guests are late (or the oven too hot) just add a little stock or water or cream around the edge of the casserole just before serving. Remember this dish is already cooked and only needs to be thoroughly re-heated.

Partridge, Snipe & Woodcock

Partridge September 1st – February 1st
Snipe August 12th – January 31st
Woodcock October 1st – January 31st (England & Wales)
September 1st – January 31st (Scotland)

Partridge with a Pear

Kenwards, Lewes
Chef/proprietor John Kenward

1 partridge
1 conference pear – still firm
  but not like a rock!
vegetables and spices for stock
  – to include, celery, carrot,
  peeled onion, bay leaf, juniper
berry, pepper
eau de vie Poire William

Fillet the breasts and legs and remove the skin from the breasts. Trim any fat and sinews.

Break up the carcass and roast for about 30 minutes. Cover with water in a large pan with vegetables and bring to the boil. Simmer gently for about 2–3 hours. Sieve, strain and reduce to about 7 fl. oz. (200ml.).

Peel the pear, and cut down the centre to remove core.

To cook, roast the legs in a hot oven for 15 minutes, at the same time fry the breasts in a little butter and seasoning for about 3 minutes each side until fairly firm when pressed. Splash a little eau de vie into the pan and remove the breast meat to a warm plate and cover.

Pour the stock into a pan and add the pear. Poach gently, turning several times until soft. The pear should be cooked through to achieve maximum flavour and the cooking time will have to be judged carefully according to the ripeness of the pear. Remove the pear to a warm plate, reduce stock, and whisk in a little butter. Check the seasoning. The sauce should be approaching a thick but still runny consistency.

To serve, arrange the whole breasts and pears on a plate with the vegetables and pour the sauce around the meat and a little over the pear.

Partridge "Karen Marie"

Le Coq Hardi, Dublin
Chef/proprietor John Howard

Serves 1

1 partridge
salt and freshly ground pepper
4 tablespoons of butter
4 oz. (125g.) pork
12 muscatel grapes
1 teaspoon eau de vie de
  Muscat
1 tablespoon port
2 tablespoons good game
  stock

Truss the partridge.

Clean and season the partridge with salt and pepper. Rub the skin with butter and cover with the pork cut into strips. Roast for 10 minutes at 400F/200C/Gas 6. Add the grapes and roast for a further 10 minutes.

Take the bird from the oven and remove the pork and truss and string. Transfer to a serving dish and keep warm.

Glaze the roasting dish with the eau de vie and the port, add the game stock and reduce the sauce. Strain.

Coat the partridge with the sauce and the grapes.

Breasts of Partridge in Puff Pastry with Wild Mushroom and Fresh Goose Liver

The Royal Crescent Hotel, Bath
Chef Michael Croft

Serves 4

2 whole partridge
1 shallot, chopped
bayleaf
thyme
3 oz. (75g.) fresh goose liver, marinated in red wine and Madeira
8 oz. (225g.) chicken mousseline
4 oz. (125g.) raw mixed wild mushrooms, roughly sliced
1 whole truffle
5 fl. oz. (150ml.) game stock
5 fl. oz. (150ml.) veal stock
5 fl. oz. (150ml.) water
pig's caul
puff pastry

Season the partridge and seal in a very hot oven for 5–8 minutes. Remove and cool. Remove the breasts and set aside.

Chop the carcass finely and sauté in a roasting pan until browned. Add a chopped shallot, bayleaf and thyme and sweat for 5 minutes. Deglaze with the fois gras marinade and a little extra Madeira. Reduce and then add the game and veal stock and the water. Cook for 15 minutes. Pass through a fine chinoise and then a muslin. Reduce down to 5 fl. oz. (150ml.). Finish by whisking in pieces of butter and passing through a fine sieve.

Sauté the wild mushrooms quickly in hot butter and cool. Bind loosely together with the chicken mousse.

Lay out small rectangles of caul and in the centre place a tablespoon of mousse and a sliced partridge breast. Add a slice of fois gras and a thick slice of truffle. Wrap the whole thing tightly in the caul. Then carefully in puff pastry. Decorate attractively and make a small hole in the centre for the sauce. Cook in the oven just long enough to cook the mousse and pastry. Serve with the sauce separately.

Oeufs de Caille ou Nid de Perdrix

Restaurant Bosquet, Kenilworth
Chef/proprietor Bernard Lignier

Serves 4

1 partridge, boned and flesh
  removed
1 egg
7 oz. (200g.) fresh cream
12 quail eggs
demi-glace
truffles, sliced and reserved in
  hot butter
game stock
brandy

Mince and sieve the meat from the bird and place in the fridge till cold. When cold add the egg and cream and salt and pepper.

Make a game stock with the bones and using the demi-glace and brandy make a rich game sauce.

Make 4 nests by selecting 8 moulds of 2 different sizes. Generously butter the large mould inside and the smaller one on the outside. Cover the inside of the large mould with 1" (2.5cm.) of mousse and place the small mould inside it. Cook in a bain-marie at 400F/200C/Gas 6 for 8 minutes. During the cooking of the nests, poach the quail eggs in simmering water – 1 pint (570ml.) and 1 sherry glass vinegar. Reserve the eggs in cold water.

Take the nests out of the moulds, place on a warm plate, fill with three quail eggs, warmed up in boiling water, and pour the sauce over. Sprinkle with truffles.

Breast of Snipe with Sloe Gin and Junipers

Corse Lawn House Hotel, Corse Lawn
Chef/proprietor Baba Hine

3 snipes per person
butter
sloe gin
juniper berries
heart shaped croutons to
    decorate
sprigs of parsley, to decorate

For the stock:

1 onion
1 leek
1 stick celery
3 carrots
bouquet garni

Bone and skin the breast of snipe and reserve.

Make a stock by browning the onion, leek, celery and carrots. Add the snipe carcases and the bouquet garni and cover with water. Simmer for a few hours until reduced to a rich stock.

Sauté the breasts of snipe for a few minutes only in butter. Remove from pan and keep warm. Make the sauce by adding equal amounts of stock and sloe gin with a pinch of crushed juniper to the pan in which you cooked the snipe breasts and reduce over high heat until syrupy.

Arrange the snipe breasts on a plate, pour the sauce around and serve garnished with a heart shaped crouton and sprigs of parsley.

Salmis de Bécasse aux Trois Choux

Le Poulbot, London
Chef Rowley Leigh

4 woodcock
18 fl. oz. (500ml.) veal stock
1 glass Madeira
1 large celeriac
½ red cabbage
8 chestnuts
1 apple
1 onion
1 lb. (450g.) choucroute
8 oz. (250g.) pork fat
1 glass white wine
thyme
6 juniper berries
1 lb. (450g.) brussel sprouts
hazelnuts

Line a caserole with slices of pork fat, add the washed and drained choucroute, the thyme, the white wine and the juniper berries. Seal well and cook in the oven until tender (1 – 2 hours).

Slice the red cabbage and onion very finely and cook in hot butter. Add a little vinegar, the peeled and chopped apple and the peeled chestnuts and cook until tender (1 hour).

Cook the chopped celeriac in a little milk and make a good purée.

Peel the outer leaves of the sprouts, slice the hearts finely and sauté in very hot butter for 2–3 minutes. Add the sliced hazelnuts and remove from the stove. Keep warm.

Truss the woodcock by placing the beak through the tail and roast in a very hot oven for 12 minutes. Allow to cool slightly and then joint each bird into 4 sections. Keep the tail meat on one side. Chop the carcasses moistened with the Madeira and veal stock and cook for 15 minutes. Pass the stock through a conical sieve, add half the tail meat and a little butter and liquidise. Correct the seasoning.

To finish, place a little of the purée in the centre of each plate and assemble the warmed pieces of woodcock in an attractive pattern on top. Surround with little pieces of the cabbages and coat generously with the sauce.

Bécasse Rôtie au Vinaigre de Framboise et Chocolat

Restaurant Bosquet, Kenilworth
Chef/proprietor Bernard Lignier

1 woodcock per person
2 shallots
1½ oz. (40g.) back fat
1 piece toast per bird
1 tablespoon brandy
2 oz. (50g.) butter
1½ oz. (40g.) foie gras or
   chicken liver

For the sauce:

1 sherry glass raspberry
   vinegar
1 sherry glass port
2 sherry glasses of demi-glace
½ oz. (15g.) bitter chocolate
1 oz. (25g.) butter

Cover the woodcock with a thin layer of back fat, pinch the legs together with the beak, season and cook in a hot oven for 5 minutes. Discard the back fat, remove the guts and reserve them (discarding the gizzard) and return the bird to the oven for a further 5 minutes. It should be pink inside.

Make the rotie by liquidising the guts with the butter, shallots, brandy, salt and pepper and foie gras or chicken liver. When smooth, place on a slice of bread, toasted on both sides, and grill slowly.

Make the sauce by boning the bird and placing the breasts and legs on the toasted rotie with the head of the bird split in two. Place the left over bones in the roasting dish, deglaze with the raspberry vinegar, port and demi-glace. Stir in the chocolate and bring to the boil and reduce by half. Pass through a fine sieve and add the butter.

Pigeon

No close season

Salad of Pigeon Breasts, Mange-touts, Grapefruit and Sherry Vinegar

L'Escargot, London
Chef Martin Lam

Serves 4

2 pigeons, breast only,
    marinated overnight in equal
    parts dry sherry and olive oil
1 curly endive
1 head raddiccio
½ lb. (225g.) mange-touts,
    lightly cooked
1 bunch chives, finely chopped
2 pink grapefruit, segmented
2 tablespoons sherry vinegar
4 tablespoons double cream
salt and black pepper

Make a salad bed of the raddiccio, curly endive and mange-touts on each plate, alternating the colours to good effect. Then lay the grapefruit segments around the outside in a cartwheel effect. This can be done in advance.

In a frying pan, sauté the pigeon breasts in butter for about 5 minutes or so. They should be just pink inside. Remove from the pan. Deglaze the pan with sherry vinegar and a splash of the marinade. Reduce by half and add the cream. Boil and reduce to a coating consistency.

Slice the pigeon breasts horizontally and lay on the salad. Grind over black pepper and sprinkle on a little salt. Pour over the hot sauce and sprinkle with chopped chives. Serve with a Gewurztraminer.

Pigeon Breast with Spinach and Ginger

Kenwards, Lewes
Chef/proprietor John Kenward

1 wood pigeon
8 oz. (225g.) spinach (true
   spinach not beat)
spices and vegetables for
   stock, to include onion, garlic,
   celery, carrot, bay leaf,
   pepper
ginger
a little dry cider
fresh root ginger

Fillet the breast of pigeon, removing the skin, and marinade in cider and bruised ginger and a little seasoning for at least 12 hours.

In a very hot oven, roast the carcass, still including the legs and wings, till brown – about ¾ of an hour. Fry the diced vegetables in a little butter and add the carcass, cover with water. Simmer gently for about 4 hours. Sieve, strain and reduce stock to about 7 fl. oz. (200ml.).

Cut the spinach into ribbons and cut a few slivers of peeled ginger. Crush a little garlic and mix together.

Fry the pigeon breasts on a medium heat for about 2–3 minutes on each side. The breasts should be soft (i.e. not cooked through) when pressed. Remove to a warmed covered plate.

De-glaze the pan with the stock and a little cider. Reduce and whisk in a little butter. Season if necessary.

Slice the pigeon breasts, not across the grain, but at a slight angle off the length.

In a very hot pan, melt some butter with a few drops of cider and toss the spinach and ginger mixture very rapidly and briefly – only seconds. Pile the mixture onto a plate, fan out the breast meat and pour the sauce around – not over or it will flatten the spinach. Under cooking is very important for both pigeon and spinach in this recipe otherwise contrasts of flavour, texture and colour will suffer.

Breast of Squab Pigeon with Braised Oakleaf Lettuce and Girolles

Partners 23, Sutton
Chef/Proprietor Tim McEntire

Serves 4

4 squab pigeon
4 oz. (125g.) fresh girolles
4 small heads of oakleaf lettuce
5 fl. oz. (150ml.) double cream
1 egg white
1 orange
1 measure Grand Marnier
1½ pts. (900ml.) game stock
unsalted butter
salt and black pepper

Remove the supremes and thighs from each pigeon.

Make a mousse with the thigh meat, cream and egg white plus the blanched and chopped zest. Season.

Remove the fillet from the breast and slightly flatten. Pipe the mousse along the breast and cover with the fillet, season with salt and pepper.

Brown the pigeon carcasses and trimmings, add the game stock, skim and simmer.

Carefully seal the filled supremes in hot fat. Add the girolles and lettuce heads, saving 4 small leaves to garnish. Cover with the strained stock and Grand Marnier. Poach until cooked with the lid on.

Remove everything from the stock and keep warm. Rapidly reduce the stock until syrupy. Finish with small cubes of unsalted butter whisked in. Check seasoning.

Serve the supremes on a bed of lettuce, scatter the girolles and coat with the sauce. Finish with the crisp centre leaf of the lettuce.

Breast of Wood Pigeon with Wild Mushrooms

Bodysgallen Hall, Llandudno
Chef David Harding

Serves 4

4 pigeons, dressed
8 oz. (225g.) wild mushrooms
½ onion, chopped
1 carrot, chopped
1 stick celery, chopped
bay leaf
thyme
1 tablespoon tomato purée
1 pint (570ml.) chicken stock
1 miniature bottle brandy
little oil
salt and black pepper

Remove the breasts from the birds and put to one side. Roughly chop the remains of the carcass and legs. Quickly fry in a hot frying pan with chopped vegetables until brown. Add the tomato purée and cook for a further 2 minutes. Add the brandy and flame. Add the chicken stock and herbs, bring to the simmer and reduce by two thirds. When this has been achieved strain through a fine strainer and season with salt or pepper to taste. Keep warm.

Quickly sauté the seasoned breasts in a hot pan for approximately 1 minute each side – remove and allow to rest.

Meanwhile, add a little more oil to the pan and quickly fry the washed and seasoned mushrooms until brown.

Arrange the pigeon breasts on a warm serving dish, coat with the sauce and the wild mushrooms. Serve immediately.

Warm Brioche of Pigeon Breast with Red Cabbage

Restaurant Roger Burdell, Loughborough
Chef/proprietor Roger Burdell

Serves 4

4 pigeon breasts
4 brioche buns, to favourite
   recipe or bought
thyme
salt and pepper
amontillado sherry
double cream
currants
stock or meat glaze
crisp bacon lardons
mushrooms, sautéed
currants
cooked red cabbage, to a
   traditional recipe
watercress or chives, to garnish

This dish is in essence simply an assembly of four separate food constituents, each requiring preparation following traditional methods.

Make the required number of brioche buns, using any of the various recipes available – alternatively purchase them from your quality bakery.

Make the red cabbage by following any of the traditional recipes, using apples, onions, wine, vinegar, chicken stock, sugar, bay leaf, juniper berries, cloves, salt and pepper.

Take the pigeon breast off the carcass, season with salt, pepper and thyme. Sauté the breasts, one each per person for a first course, and reserve in a warm place.

To make the sauce, deglaze the pan with the sherry, add double cream and reduce by approximately half. Add the meat glaze or simple stock, and the currants, bacon lardons and sautéed mushrooms.

To assemble, spoon a ring of red cabbage onto each plate. Slice the pigeon breasts thinly and arrange over the cabbage in a circle. Cut off the top of the warm brioche and scoop out some of the soft middle. Place the bottom half of the brioche in the centre of each plate. Spoon the bacon currants, mushrooms and some of the sauce into the brioche and replace the lid. Spoon the remainder of the sauce over the sliced pigeon breasts. Garnish with watercress or chives.

33

Squab with Thyme and Sweet Garlic

Thackeray's House Restaurant, Tunbridge Wells
Chef/proprietor Bruce Wass

Serves 2

2 squabs (young pigeon)
12 large garlic cloves, peeled
2 large garlic cloves, unpeeled
½ lemon
1 teaspoon coarse seasalt
12 crushed peppercorns
1 large bunch fresh thyme
½ glass white wine
5 fl. oz. (150ml.) strong veal
   stock, flavoured with the
   squab giblets

One day in advance, chop the unpeeled garlic and half a lemon, and mix together with the crushed peppercorns, sea salt and some chopped thyme. Stuff the squabs with this mixture and lightly truss.

Next day season the squabs till brown in butter and cook for approximately 15 minutes.

Meanwhile blanch and refresh the peeled garlic cloves in cold water (twice if new season, three times if not).

In the pot that the pigeons were cooked, sauté the garlic cloves until golden brown with a little chopped thyme. When brown place into another pot with a teaspoon of sugar, a pinch of salt and cover with stock. Simmer for 5 minutes and then boil fast until the stock evaporates and the garlic is glazed. Keep warm.

In the pot that the pigeons were cooked, add a glass of white wine, reduce by half and add the stock and reduce that by half as well.

Joint the squab and arrange on a plate with the garlic cloves. Squeeze all the juice out of the carcass into the sauce and whisk in a little fresh butter. Pour over the squabs.

Wood Pigeon in Two Sauces

Fischer's, Bakewell
Chef/proprietor Max Fischer

Serves 4

4 wood pigeon
pork back fat
salt and black pepper

For the port wine sauce:

bones from wood pigeon
2 shallots, finely chopped
½ pint (275ml.) white wine
1 fl. oz. (25ml.) brandy
1 fl. oz. (25ml.) port
sprigs of thyme and rosemary
10 peppercorns
½ bayleaf
butter

For the wild mushrooms:

8 oz. (225g.) wild mushrooms
2 shallots, finely chopped
salt and black pepper
unsalted butter
1 fl. oz. (25ml.) white port
1 cup crème fraiche
chives, freshly chopped

Season the wood pigeon and cover the breasts with fat. Roast in the oven keeping the meat pink. Set aside to cool. Bone out.

For the port wine sauce, chop the pigeon bones and return to the roasting tin. Add the shallots and sweat. De-glaze with white wine, brandy and port. Add the thyme, peppercorns, bay leaf and rosemary. Bring to the boil and simmer for 5 minutes. Strain and reduce to half the quantity. To finish, whisk in little knobs of butter.

For the wild mushroom sauce, sweat the shallots in butter. Add the mushrooms and seasoning. Toss the mushrooms and remove from the pan. De-glaze the pan with the white port, add the crème fraiche and reduce slightly. Return the mushrooms to the pan and garnish with the chives.

To serve, arrange half the pigeon breasts on one side of the platter and spoon over the port wine sauce. Arrange the mushroom sauce the other side of the platter, and display the remaining wood pigeon on this.

Pigeon with Lovage in Perry Sauce

Hope End, Ledbury
Chef/proprietor Patricia Hegarty

Serves 6

6 plump spring pigeons
2 tablespoons sunflower oil
1 medium onion, chopped
2 pints (1.1 lt.) dry perry
   (preferably Dunkertons)
small bunch lovage
salt and pepper
tamari
2 teaspoons cornflour

Use the oil to brown the breasts of the pigeon.

Put the pigeons head down in a casserole. Add the onion and cover the pigeons with the perry. If necessary top up with a little water. Tuck a few lovage leaves down the side of the pot. Cook slowly at 300F/150C/Gas 2 for 2½ to 3 hours until the birds are really tender. Take out and cool.

Keep about 1 pint (570ml.) of the cooking juices warm in the casserole.

Strain the remainder of the cooking juices and reduce to about ½ pint (275ml.). Taste and add a few more lovage leaves if you like it stronger. Thicken this sauce with the cornflour. Strain. Finally season with salt and pepper and a dash of tamari.

Remove the breasts from the pigeons and replace them in the casserole to warm in a low oven.

When ready to serve quickly drain each breast on a piece of kitchen paper, spoon over the sauce and garnish with a bright green lovage leaf.

Pheasant

October 1st – February 1st

Salad of Pheasant with Celeriac and Citrus Sauce Dressing

Woods, Bicester
Chef/proprietor Robert Harrison

Serves 2

legs and breasts of a pheasant,
 boned
3½ fl. oz. (100ml.) citrus fruit
 juices
1 tablespoon Madeira
knob of butter
1 tablespoon cream
seasonal salad and herbs
favourite salad dressing, using
 walnut oil
few walnuts
½ small celeriac, trimmed, cut
 into matchsticks and lightly
 dressed with lemon

Sauté the pheasants, well seasoned, until just pink. Remove from the pan and keep warm.

Add the citrus juice to the pan and reduce by ½. Add the Madeira and cream and reduce till lightly syrupy. Whisk in the butter.

Slice the pheasant meat and roll the pieces in the citrus sauce with some chopped herbs. Arrange on plates around the salad and place the celeriac on top.

Roast Pheasant with White Grapes, Armagnac and Morrilles

Marlfield House, Gorey
Chef/proprietor Mary Bowe

Serves 4–6

2 medium sized pheasants
4 slices bacon
mirepoix of vegetables
1 tablespoon tomato purée
bouquet garni
small bunch seedless white
   grapes
1 large glass Armagnac
5–6 morrilles, chopped
½ pint (275ml.) cream

Make a stock by removing the winglets and the giblets from the pheasants. Sauté in a saucepan with the mirepoix of vegetables, a spoonful of tomato purée and a bouquet garni. Add 2 pints (1.1 litres) cold water and simmer for ¾ hour.

Season the pheasant and place 2 slices of bacon on each bird – this will ensure that the breasts keep moist. Place in a roasting tray and cook in a pre-heated oven at 400F/220C/Gas 6 for between 30 to 45 minutes, depending upon which way you like your pheasant cooked.

Make the sauce by sweating off the chopped morrilles in butter. Add the Armagnac and reduce by half. Add 1 pint (570ml.) of the pheasant stock. Simmer for 10 minutes. Finally add the cream and the seedless grapes. Season to taste.

Roast Pheasant with Celery and Bacon

The Wife of Bath, Wye
Chef/proprietor Bob Johnson

Serves 8

2 young pheasant, well hung
1 head celery, chopped
1 lb. (450g.) bacon, chopped
half cup port
1 cup cream
salt and black pepper
butter

Season the birds and brown on both sides. Put into a deep sided roasting dish, cover with the celery, bacon and port and roast for about 40 minutes in a hot oven. Turn the pheasant once during the cooking process. When the birds are just cooked remove and keep warm.

Add the cream to the juices in the pan and boil again until a rich creamy consistency is obtained. Check seasoning.

Cut the pheasant into portions and pour the sauce over. Roast potatoes and a green salad are all that is needed to serve with this dish.

Supreme of Pheasant with Almonds

Buckland Manor, Buckland
Chef Martyn Pearn

Serves 4

4 pheasant breasts
2 oz. (50g.) toasted and flaked
  almonds
4 oz. (125g.) butter
6 fl. oz. (175ml.) ruby port
18 fl. oz. (500ml.) veal stock
2 tablespoons meat glaze
salt and pepper

Season the pheasant breasts and roast in butter till pink. Remove and set aside to keep warm.

Glaze the pan with the port and add the meat glaze. Reduce and then add the veal stock. Reduce again by half. Check seasoning.

To serve, re-heat the breasts and slice into two. Sprinkle on the almonds and coat with the sauce.

Sautéed Breast of Pheasant with Girolles, Foie Gras and Grapes

Restaurant Seventy Four, Canterbury
Chef/proprietor I. L. McAndrew

Serves 4

2 pheasants, breasts removed

3 oz. (75g.) girolles, carefully cleaned to remove dirt, but not washed

5 oz. (150g.) white grapes, peeled and de-seeded

2 oz. (50g.) fresh foie gras, cut into dice ¼" (0.5cm)

3 fl. oz. (75ml.) dry white wine

10 fl. oz. (275ml.) thickened pheasant stock

2 oz. (50g.) butter

½ tablespoon oil

Heat the oil in a suitable pan, add about half of the butter and allow to sizzle. Season the breasts of pheasants and place in the pan and gently cook on one side until lightly browned. Turn and complete the cooking again and only lightly brown. When cooked, remove the breasts from the pan and keep in a warm place.

Return the pan to the heat and add the girolles, lightly season and toss in the pan until cooked. When almost cooked add the grapes and toss along with the girolles. Drain the grapes and mushrooms from the pan, and keep warm.

Take the fat out of the pan, and over a high heat add the white wine and reduce until almost gone. Add the pheasant stock and bring to the boil. Reduce until it thickens.

When ready to serve, place the breasts of pheasant in a hot oven for a minute to reheat. Gradually add the remaining butter and sauce whisking continuously until it is all melted. Season the diced foie gras, and quickly fry in a hot frying pan for a couple of seconds. Add the girolles and grapes and toss together until hot.

Place a pile of the girolles mixture just off the centre of each plate, slice each pheasant breast into six slices and lay on the plate next to the girolles. Strain the sauce through a fine strainer and pour over and around the pheasant.

Breast of Pheasant Forestière

Gravetye Manor, East Grinstead
Chef Allan Garth

Serves 4

2 pheasants
8 oz. (225g.) wild mushrooms,
   picked and washed
½ pint (275ml.) double cream
½ pint (275ml.) game sauce
1 tablespoon brandy
6 tablespoons double cream
salt and pepper
1 egg
pine kernels to garnish

Remove the breasts and the legs from the pheasants. Take the meat from the thighs and retain.

To make the mousse, pass the thigh meat through the fine blade of a mincer twice. Put the meat into a bowl over ice and beat in the egg, salt and pepper, making sure the meat stays very cold or the mousse will split. The mixture should now be quite rubbery. Beat in the brandy and the double cream and correct the seasoning. Butter 4 small tumblers, and fill with mousse. Cook in a bain-marie for about 10 minutes at 375F/190C/Gas 5.

To make the sauce, reduce the cream and game sauce by half. Sauté the wild mushrooms lightly. Strain and add to the reduced sauce. Keep warm.

Sauté the seasoned breasts of pheasant in a pan until coloured. Place into a very hot oven for about 5 minutes, depending upon the size of the breasts. When cooked the pheasant should be pink inside.

Slice the pheasant breasts and place onto four plates. Cover with the sauce. Take out the mousses and sprinkle the pheasant with pine kernels.

Breast of Pheasant filled with Pheasant and Whisky Pâté in a Madeira and Cream Sauce

The Old Monastery, Drybridge
Chef/proprietor Douglas Craig

Serves 4

2 young pheasants, dressed
egg wash
flour
fresh brown breadcrumbs

For the pâtè:

2 oz. (50g.) smoked streaky
    bacon
4 oz. (125g.) chicken livers
4 oz. (125g.) flesh from the
    pheasant legs
1 fl. oz. (25ml.) Amontillado
    sherry
½ fl. oz. (15ml.) whisky
2 oz. (50g.) butter
pinch thyme
pinch mixed spice
½ clove garlic

A young hen pheasant when roasted to perfection is undoubtedly the finest way to enjoy this superb bird, but in an à la carte restaurant specialising in 'cooked to order' this excludes roast pheasant from the menu as few customers are prepared to wait long enough for its preparation. This recipe is a successful attempt at adapting a chicken recipe so that the pheasant is cooked to order – most of the hard work for this recipe can be carried out well in advance!

Remove the legs and breasts from the birds. Remove the skin from the breasts and legs, trim fat from the breasts. Set the breasts aside and separate the thighs from the drumsticks. Remove the bone from the thighs.

Make a stock by placing the carcass, bones and drumsticks in a roasting tin in a moderate oven till browned. Transfer to a suitable pot, add the vegetables and the water and bring to the boil. Simmer for 4 hours.

Make a pâté by sautéing the thigh flesh in ½ oz. (15g.) butter with the lid on for 7 minutes. Add the herb, spice and garlic and cook for a further minute. Remove flesh to the food processor. Sauté the chopped bacon in the same pan and transfer to processor. Whizz till finely minced. Deglaze the cooking pan with sherry and add to the food processor. Melt the remainder of the butter and add to the processor and give a further spin. Add the whisky and check seasoning. Set aside to cool and solidify.

For the sauce:

15 fl. oz. (400ml.) game stock
1 fl. oz. (25ml.) sercial Madeira
2 shallots, chopped
½ oz. (15g.) butter
6 fl. oz. (175ml.) double cream

For the game stock:

pheasant carcass and
    trimmings
1 onion, sliced
1 carrot, sliced
2 sticks celery, sliced
bouquet garni
1½ pints (900ml.) water
little oil

Prepare the breasts for filling by removing the fillets from the breasts and flatten carefully without splitting the meat. Make a cavity in the underside of the breast with a sharp knife. Fill the cavity with pâté, wet the flesh around the edge, flour one side of the fillet and place the floured side uppermost on top of the pâté. Fold over the moistened flaps to form a seal. This can be prepared several hours before required.

Dip the breasts in flour, egg wash and seasoned breadcrumbs and deep fry in very hot oil for 10–12 minutes.

Make the sauce by sweating the shallots in ½ oz. (15g.) of butter. Add the game stock, reduce by half and strain into a fresh pan. Add the Madeira and cream and continue to reduce until the sauce thickens slightly. Check seasoning.

Pheasant Breast with Snails

The Country Garden, Ashburton
Chef/proprietor Hassan El-Masri

Serves 4

4 pheasant breasts
24 burgundy snails
1 oz. (25g.) butter
2 shallots
1 fl. oz. (25ml.) cognac
4 oz. (125g.) button mushrooms
4 fl. oz. (125ml.) cream
2 egg yolks
chives, to garnish

Cut the pheasant breasts into strips, season and sauté in butter with shallots and sliced mushrooms – do not allow to colour.

When the pheasant is tender add the cognac and de-glaze the pan.

Add the snails and the cream and beat in 2 egg yolks to thicken the sauce. Decorate with chopped chives and serve.

Pheasant in Pastry with Pâté and Mushrooms

The Carved Angel, Dartmouth
Chef/proprietor Joyce Molyneux

12 oz. (350g.) short crust pastry
1 whole pheasant
liver pâté, made with chicken,
    goose, duck or pheasant liver
    (already made or bought)
equal quantities of belly pork
    and thigh meat from
    pheasant
Madeira

For the duxelles:

4 oz. (125g.) mushrooms,
chopped
1 small onion, chopped
2 oz. (50g.) butter
salt and pepper

Make a duxelles in the usual way, by melting the butter in a pan and cooking the mushroom and onion til dry – stirring all the time to prevent burning.

Take the legs and breast off the pheasant and make a stock with the bones.

Slice each breast into 4 and season.

Take the meat off the thighs and mince with an equal amount of salt belly pork. Season the mixture and add 2 tablespoons of Madeira.

Roll out the shortcrust pastry into a long oblong and spread some of the duxelles mixture on it. Next spread some thigh/pork mix onto the duxelles and then place some slices of pheasant breast on top. Finish with a little pâté. Then place on more breast, thigh/pork mix and duxelles. Fold the pastry over, seal the joints and brush with egg wash. Roast for ½ hour in a hot oven.

Make a sauce by reducing the stock to a very small amount. Add some Madeira and check seasoning. Finish by whisking in a few small cubes of butter.

Suprème de Faisan en Croûte

Stane Street Hollow, Pulborough
Chef/Proprietor Rene Kaiser

Serves 4

2 pheasants
8 slices smoked bacon
8 oz. (225g.) puff pastry
salt and pepper
1 egg

For the duxelles:

1 medium onion, sliced
1 clove garlic, crushed
8 juniper berries, crushed and
    chopped
8 oz. (225g.) mushrooms
thyme and marjoram

Skin the 2 pheasants and remove the breasts. Slice the breasts open along the middle to make a pocket. Season with salt and pepper.

Make the duxelles by frying the chopped onion, sliced mushrooms, crushed garlic and juniper berries and herbs in a little fat for 2 to 3 minutes. Leave to cool and chop fairly finely.

Divide the duxelles mixture equally and stuff into the pheasant breasts. Close the opening and wrap each breast with 2 slices of bacon.

Roll out the puff pastry and cut into 4" x 8" (10cm. x 20cm.) squares and wrap each breast individually. Coat each parcel with a little beaten egg in a medium oven for 20 to 25 minutes.

Pheasant Braised with Lentils

Gidleigh Park, Chagford
Chef Shaun Hill

Serves 4

2 pheasants
8 oz. (225g.) brown lentils
8 oz. (225g.) streaky bacon, chopped
4 oz. (125g.) celery, chopped
8 oz. (225g.) carrots, chopped
1 onion, chopped
2 oz. (50g.) butter
2 fl. oz. (50ml.) red wine
5 fl. oz. (150ml.) game or chicken stock
2 cloves garlic, chopped

Wash the lentils through two or three changes of water – take care to pick out any little stones. Boil in salt water till tender – about 5–10 minutes.

Half roast the pheasants and set aside. Deglaze the cooking juices with the red wine.

Sauté the bacon, celery, carrots, garlic and onion. Add the lentils and stock. Bring to the boil and reduce till thickened. Add the jointed pheasant and cover the pan with buttered paper. Cook in the oven for 30 minutes till moist and cooked. Check salt.

Quail

No close season

Cold Roast Quail Salad

Bowlish House, Shepton Mallet
Proprietors Julia and Brian Jordan

3 cold, roasted quail
1 ripe mango, sliced
1 ripe avocado, sliced
3 rashers smoked back bacon,
  sliced
12 quails eggs
a selection of chopped mixed
  continental lettuces

For the dressing:

4 tablespoons olive oil
1 tablespoon tarragon vinegar
1 tablespoon fresh tarragon,
  finely chopped
1 tablespoon Meaux mustard
1 teaspoon caster sugar
salt and pepper

Cook the bacon until brown and crisp, and leave to cool and cut into fine strips about 1" (2.5cm.) long.

Poach the quail eggs in simmering water for 2 minutes and then plunge into iced water.

Slice the meat off the quails.

Wash the lettuce and arrange a pile in the centre of each plate.

Place the avocado, mango, roast quail and bacon into a bowl and toss with tarragon dressing.

Arrange over the lettuce and top each portion with 2 poached quails eggs.

Quail in Aspic

The Carved Angel, Dartmouth
Chef/proprietor Joyce Molyneux

3 quail
6 quail eggs
parsley
nutmeg
double cream
Madeira
egg white
chicken stock

For the aspic:

1 lb. (450g.) raw chicken giblets
   and carcass
1 pigs trotter
2 oz. (50g.) carrot
1 piece of celery
parsley stalks, sprig of thyme
   and bay leaf
4 oz. (125g.) onions, unpeeled
12 peppercorns
2 pints (generous litre) cold
   water

Place the ingredients for the aspic in a pan, bring to the boil and simmer gently for 4 hours. Strain and set aside.

To clarify, heat the liquid with beaten egg white, when it boils strain through muslin. Season to taste – it should be fairly highly seasoned.

Boil the quail eggs for 3 minutes. Cool under cold tap and shell. Slice eggs in half.

To make the quail mousse. Remove the legs from the quail, bone and weigh them. To each 4 oz. (125g.) meat, allow 1½ egg whites and 3½ fl. oz. (100ml.) cream. Purée the egg white and meat in a liquidiser and put through a fine sieve. Whip the cream lightly and gradually beat it into the purée. Season with salt, pepper, nutmeg and a little Madeira. Poach the mousse by dropping teaspoons of it into simmering, seasoned chicken stock for about 5 minutes. Drain and dry on kitchen paper. Allow to cool.

Roast the now legless quails, with gut still intact, in a hot oven for not more than 20 minutes. Allow to cool, detach breasts and skin. Slice thinly.

To assemble, first ensure that the ingredients are cold. In small aluminium moulds or a single dish, put a layer of halved quail eggs, then a layer of sliced breasts, and then mousseline. Each layer must be set in aspic before the next is added. Chopped parsley in each layer will add colour. The inclusion of the pigs trotter should mean that the aspic should set without any problem, but patience (and a good refrigerator) is a virtue. Metal moulds can be turned out easily if held under the hot tap for 2 seconds. Accompany with apple mayonnaise.

For the apple mayonnaise, sweat a chopped cooking apple in butter. Sieve into a purée and when cool beat into your home made mayonnaise. This deliciously refreshing sauce is served with the dish at our restaurant.

A Rendezvous of Quail on a Crispy Salad

Partners 23, Sutton
Chef/proprietor Tim McEntire

Serves 4

4 fresh quail
8 quails eggs
freshly picked salad leaves
   (eg. corn salad, curly endive,
   oakleaf lettuce, red lettuce,
   green batavia)
3 oz. (75g.) streaky bacon
toasted pine kernels
dressing, made with nut oil and
   red wine vinegar
Hollandaise or butter sauce

For the mousse:

3 oz. (75g.) quail livers
1 egg white
4 fl. oz. (125ml.) double cream

Make a mousse from the livers, egg white and cream. Gently steam in 4 buttered moulds until cooked.

Roast the quails in a hot oven.

Prick each egg once with a pin and plunge into boiling water for 130 secs. Refresh quickly in iced water. Carefully shell.

Break up the large leaves of salad, wash and dry. Toss in a little light nut oil dressing. Arrange on plates.

Cut the quails into 4 and arrange on top of the individual salads. Turn out a mousse on the front of each salad.

Re-heat the eggs in boiling water for about 30 seconds and place on salad. Coat the mousse and eggs with a little butter sauce or hollandaise. Finish with snippets of crispy fried bacon and toasted pine kernels.

Roast Quail with Grapes

Michael's, Bristol
Chef/proprietor Michael McGowan

Serves 4

8 quails
4 tablespoons brandy
4 oz. (125g.) grapes, peeled
  and deseeded
8 vine leaves (optional), soaked
  in brandy
1 rasher streaky bacon per bird
2 rashers back bacon, finely
  chopped
livers from the quails or 4 oz.
  (125g.) chicken livers, finely
  chopped
2 oz. (50g.) mushrooms, finely
  chopped
4 oz. (125g.) butter
white breadcrumbs
salt and black pepper
8 heart-shaped croutons of
  fried bread

Mix the chopped livers with the bacon and mushrooms. Add half the brandy and enough breadcrumbs to form a moist stuffing. Fill the cavities of the birds with this mixture.

Wrap the quails in the vine leaves which have been soaked in brandy and then wrap the birds in the streaky bacon. Place the birds in a baking tray, brush with molten butter and sprinkle with a little salt and pepper. Place in a hot oven for 10–15 minutes until lightly browned.

Take out the birds and turn the oven down to 300–350F/150–180C Gas 2–4. Flame the birds with the rest of the brandy, add the butter and cover with foil. Return to the oven for a further 5–10 minutes.

To serve, place 2 heart shaped croutons on each plate and place a quail on top of each crouton. Add the grapes to the pan juices and swirl over heat to form a sauce (add a little more brandy if necessary to bring the sauce together). Pour over the birds and serve with plain boiled potatoes, pasta or rice and a green salad.

Roast Quail with Smokey Bacon

The Country Garden, Ashburton
Chef/proprietor Hassan El-Masri

Serves 1

2 quails
3 strips of smokey bacon
1 shallot
4 small wild mushrooms
1 tablespoon whisky
2 fl. oz. (50ml.) game stock
2 fl. oz. (50ml.) chicken stock
2 croutons
4 mange-tout pods

Roast the 2 quails with the bacon over the breasts. When cooked, remove the quails and keep warm.

De-glaze the pan with the game and chicken stock and reduce by half. Add the diced shallot, wild mushroom and whisky.

Remove the bacon from the quails and add to the sauce.

Serve the quails on small fried croutons with the sauce poured over.

Garnish with lightly fried mange-tout pods.

Quail Breast in Artichoke Hearts

Billesley Manor, Billesley
Chef Michael Monahan

Serves 4

8 quails, legs removed
8 fresh artichokes, bottoms
   cooked
2 oz. (50g.) shallots, slowly
   browned in butter
3 oz. (75g.) julienne of mixed
   vegetables (blanched)
3 fl. oz. (75ml.) Madeira
½ pint (275ml.) quail stock,
   which you have made from
   the quail bones and have
   reduced by half to a quarter
   of a pint (150ml.)
2 fl. oz. (50ml.) truffle juice
5 fl. oz. (150ml.) double cream
watercress
2 oz. (50g.) unsalted butter
salt and black pepper

Remove the legs from the quails and de-bone. Chop the leg meat into small dice.

Heat a pan until very hot and quickly sauté the leg meat to give it some colour. Add the shallots and sweat for 5 minutes.

De-glaze the pan with the Madeira and add the reduced quail stock. Add the truffle juice and the julienne of vegetables and then pour in the cream and reduce to the required consistency (the sauce should be a dark coffee colour).

Roast the quail breasts till they are pink. Rest for a few minutes then remove the breasts from the carcass.

Heat the artichoke bottoms and place two on each plate.

Heat the sauce through, remove from the heat and stir in the butter. Spoon the sauce into each artichoke and lay two quail breasts on top.

Suprème de Caille aux Raisins et Sauternes et Gateau de Foie Gras

Ortolan, Shinfield
Chef/proprietor J. W. Burton-Race

Serves 6

6 quails
4 medium shallots, sliced
1 clove garlic, chopped
8 oz. (225g.) white grapes, halved, depipped and peeled
8 white mushrooms, sliced
dash sherry vinegar
7 fl. oz. (200ml.) port
7 fl. oz. (200ml.) Madeira
¼ bottle Sauternes
3½ fl. oz. (100ml.) glace de viande
chicken stock to cover

Season the quails and seal them in a hot pan. Then roast until pink. Allow to cool, remove breasts and legs.

Chop the bones and return to the pan with the shallots, garlic, bay leaf, pepper, thyme and herb stalks and lightly sauté. Add the white mushrooms and halved grapes. Put in the oven and cook until the bones start to caramelise. Remove from the oven and deglaze the pan with the vinegar until dry. Add the port and reduce till dry and add a dash of Madeira and reduce till dry. Add the Sauternes, reduce by half, cover with chicken stock and bring to the boil. Cook gently, constantly skimming, for 40 minutes. Pass through a fine chinois, skim, reduce by half and finish with the glace de viande. Add the grapes to the sauce at the last moment.

Wash the livers, remove the gall and any discoloured parts and dry on paper. Put into a bowl, add the foie gras and beef marrow, thyme, garlic, bay leaf and the port (just enough to cover the livers), and finally add the brandy.

For the gateau:

8 oz. (225g.) chicken livers,
   soaked in milk for 12 hours
8 oz. (225g.) foie gras, chopped
   small
¼ of a bay leaf
1 clove garlic
1 sprig fresh thyme
4 oz. (125g.) beef marrow
1 pint (570ml.) cream
4 whole eggs
port
cognac
5 fl. oz. (150ml.) milk

Leave in the fridge for a minimum of 6 hours. Then remove the garlic, thyme and bay leaf and liquidise to a fine purée. Add the milk and cream to the purée, whisk until blended and then add the eggs. Season with salt and pepper and pass through a fine mesh sieve. Leave the mixture to stand for 5 minutes, then remove all the froth from the top. Pour the mixture into lightly buttered dishes and cook in a bain-marie, in the oven at 350F/180C/Gas 4 until the mixture has set.

Quails Sauteéd in Wine

Peacock Vane, Isle of Wight
Chef Rosalind Wolfenden

Serves 4

2 quails per person, dipped in
  seasoned flour
6 juniper berries, freshly ground
4 oz. (125g.) button
  mushrooms, trimmed
½ bottle red or white wine
2 oz. (50g.) butter
crouton of fried bread per bird

This recipe is very quick and requires almost no preparation. It is very suitable for home entertaining when your time is limited.

Heat the butter in a heavy bottom frying pan and brown the floured quails well on all sides. Add the mushrooms. Season with salt and pepper and sprinkle on the ground juniper berries. Pour the wine over the quails and reduce the heat so that the wine barely simmers. Cover the pan with a lid so that the liquor does not evaporate, and turn the quails once or twice during cooking.

After 20–25 minutes the quails should be cooked. Remove from cooking juices and keep warm. Reduce the cooking juices, check seasoning. Serve the quail on the croutons of fried bread with the sauce poured over.

Wild Duck

September 1st – January 31st

Hot Teal Pâté en Croûte

La Ciboulette, Cheltenham
Chef/proprietor Kevin Jenkins

2 teal, boned
1 measure port
1 measure brandy
2 egg yolks
3 fl. oz. (75ml.) double cream
salt and pepper
6 oz. (175g.) puff pastry

Place the meat from the teal in a food processor and mix for one minute. Add the egg yolks, mix again and pass through a fine sieve. Add the alcohol, salt and pepper and finally the cream.

Roll out two 3″ (7.5cm.) circles of puff pastry. Place the pâté on one circle and cover with the other using egg wash. Egg wash the top and cook in a hot oven until golden brown – about 15 minutes. Serve with a sauce of your choice – a port sauce goes particularly well.

Wild Duck with Bourbon and Apple Sauce

Pomegranates, London
Chef/proprietor Patrick Gwynn-Jones

Serves 4

4 plump hen mallards
4 apples
4 large onions, roughly
   chopped
butter
salt and black pepper
4 fl. oz. (125ml.) bourbon
   whisky
1 cup apple jelly

Clean and dry the birds inside and out.

Roughly chop 2 of the apples and mix with the onions, a large knob of softened butter, freshly ground black pepper and salt. Stuff the birds with this mixture.

Coat the outside of the birds with butter and sprinkle well with pepper and salt. Place on a rack in the roasting tray in the oven at about 425F/220C/Gas 7 and roast for 10 minutes. After 10 minutes baste the duck every few minutes with the bourbon and apple jelly which you have melted together. Continue roasting and basting until the birds have been cooking for 25 minutes. The meat should be still quite rare now. A few minutes more may be needed for some people. Place on a hot serving dish and keep warm.

Slice the remaining 2 apples and sauté in the pan juices and serve with the ducks, together with the remaining juices. Prepare seasoned wild rice with a little bacon and onion and serve with the ducks.

Colvert Roti à l'Echalotte et Vinaigre de Framboises

Le Poulbot, London
Chef Rowley Leigh

2 mallards
½ bottle red wine
½ lb. (225g.) shallots, sliced in
   fine rounds
raspberry vinegar
9 fl. oz. (250ml.) veal stock
salt and pepper

Season the mallards and roast in a hot oven for approximately 20 minutes, keeping the meat rare. Remove from oven and allow to cool slightly.

Sauté the shallots in butter. When nicely coloured, add a few drops of raspberry vinegar and half of the red wine and leave to stew for 20 minutes.

Remove the legs and breasts from the mallards and reserve. Chop the carcasses, replace in the roasting pan. Add the rest of the red wine, the veal stock and simmer for 10 minutes.

Pass the stock through a conical strainer onto the shallot mixture and reduce if necessary. Check for seasoning – the raspberry vinegar should be a very subtle presence – and add a little butter.

Warm the pieces of duck gently and cover with the sauce.

Roast Teal with Elderberry Vinegar Sauce

Morels, Haslemere
Chef/proprietor J. Morel

Serves 2

2 teal
3½ oz. (100g.) mirepoix (made
  from half a Spanish onion,
  half a carrot and half a leek
  cut into small dice)
2 shallots, peeled and chopped
½ pint (275ml.) veal stock
2 fl. oz. (50ml.) single cream
2 oz. (50g.) butter
elderberry vinegar
elderberries to decorate

You will need to find fresh elderberries for this recipe but with a little searching they should not be too hard to discover as they grow wild all over the country. If you can get them they are well worth picking and preserving. Wash them well and put into pickling jars with red wine vinegar. This will make a very dark vinegar.

Put the teal on a roasting tray and cook in a hot oven for about 5 minutes (the birds should be very pink). Take out and leave to rest for 5 minutes. Carve the birds, taking the breast, wing portions and the legs off the carcass. Put to one side and keep warm.

Chop up the carcass bones and cook in a little oil until brown. Add the mirepoix and the shallots. Deglaze the tray by adding half a cupful of elderberry vinegar and cooking so that the liquid evaporates. Add the veal stock and cream and let the mixture cook for 10 minutes. Strain the sauce and add the butter to give shine. Pour the sauce around the carved teal and decorate with elderberries.

Aiguillette de Canard Sauvage

Ortolan, Shinfield
Chef/proprietor J. W. Burton-Race

Serves 2

1 wild duck
armagnac
3 shallots, finely sliced
6 white mushrooms, finely
  sliced
clarified juice 1 orange
1 tablespoon redcurrant jelly
2 pieces orange zest
little thyme, bay leaf and garlic
ground white pepper
3½ fl. oz. (100ml.) port
7 fl. oz. (200ml.) white wine
  vinegar
2 juniper berries
18 fl. oz. (500ml.) chicken stock
11 fl. oz. (300ml.) glace de
  viande

Seal the duck in a hot pan and then set to roast in a hot oven until very pink – during the roasting process flame the bird with armagnac. Remove from the pan and leave to relax for 10 minutes. Remove the legs and breasts from the carcass and any sinew or excess fat.

Chop the bones and sauté in butter with the shallots mushrooms, herbs and the pepper. Continue to cook until golden brown – when it starts to caramelise add the redcurrant jelly. Cook out and deglaze with the orange until dry. Add the port and reduce till dry. Add the white wine and reduce by half and then add some chicken stock to cover. Bring up to the boil, skim and gently simmer for 45 minutes, skimming constantly. Pass through a fine chinois and skim again. Reduce by half and finish the sauce with the glace de viande. Correct seasoning and add a knob of butter at the last minute.

In a pan with sugar and butter, caramelise some apple segments for garnish – you can use any other fruit in season. Also good as a garnish is thinly cut duck skin, crisped in its own fat in a pan.

Wild Duck Marinated in Honey and Grapefruit with a Carrot and Ginger Purée

Bowlish House, Shepton Mallet
Proprietors Julia and Brian Jordan

Serves 4

4 breasts wild duck

For the marinade:

2 tablespoons soya sauce
1 tablespoon dry sherry
1 tablespoon olive oil
½ pint (275ml.) grapefruit juice
1 tablespoon organic honey
1 tablespoon ground mace
1 clove of garlic, crushed
1 teaspoon salt

For the purée:

8 oz. (225g.) cooked carrots
1 tablespoon chopped stem
   ginger

In a food processor, purée the carrots and stem ginger.

Make a few shallow incisions in the flesh of the duck breast and immerse in the marinade mixture for at least 12 hours. Remove from the marinade and seal both sides of each breast in a lightly oiled pan at a high temperature. After sealing leave in the pan to cook until pink.

Reduce the marinade in a separate pan and pour over the duck breasts in their pan, just prior to serving. Garnish with small mounds of the carrot and ginger purée.

Breast of Wild Duck with Caramelised Apples and Marc de Bourgogne

The Royal Crescent Hotel, Bath
Chef Michael Croft

Serves 1

1 wild duck
mirepoix of vegetables
    (eg. carrots, celery, garlic,
    leek, chopped into small dice)
1 apple, peeled and cored
2 measures Marc de
    Bourgogne
4 tablespoons duck glaze
butter
potato croquettes, rolled in
    nibbed almonds and
    breadcrumbs and studded
    with a short length of
    spaghetti, deep fried and
    finished with a sprig of mint to
    resemble an apple

Roast the duck for 30 minutes on a bed of mirepoix and herbs – make sure the duck is very pink. Place the duck on one side.

Tip off any excess fat and add 1 measure of the Marc de Bourgogne and reduce by half. Add the duck glaze and reduce by a third, season and pass through a fine sieve. Finish by whisking in small pieces of butter.

Slice the apples, sprinkle with sugar and glaze under the grill. Reheat the breasts of the duck in the oven and flame with a little of the spirit. Fan the breasts around the plate with apple slices in between and cover with the sauce. Decorate with the croquette ball in the centre.

Feuilleté of Teal with Pomerol Wine

Woods, Bicester
Chef/proprietor Robert Harrison

Serves 4

meat from teal, and the livers
8 rings flakey pastry, 4" (10cm.)
 in diameter, ⅛" (0.3cm.) thick
egg wash
brandy
1 whole egg
7 fl. oz. (200ml.) double cream
2 oz. (50g.) raw foie gras

For the red wine stock:

18 fl. oz. (500ml.) strong red
 wine
shallots, chopped
garlic, chopped
stock made from teal bones
½ bottle Pomerol wine
2 oz. (50g.) butter

Marinate the teal flesh and liver in a little brandy. Blend the flesh and liver with the egg. Push through a sieve and place over ice for 1 hour. Season and beat in the foie gras and cream.

Egg wash the edges of four of the pastry rings and divide the mousse evenly between them. Place the remaining rings on top, seal well, egg wash and decorate attractively. Bake in the oven until a dark gold and the pastry is obviously cooked. Serve with the sauce.

Make the sauce by frying the shallots and garlic in oil till golden. Add the strong red wine and reduce. Add the stock and reduce by half. Pass through a fine sieve. Add the Pomerol and reduce further till the correct consistency is obtained. Whisk in a little butter and check seasoning.

Hare & Rabbit

Rabbit No close season
Hare No close season,
but should not be offered for sale
during March to July, inclusive

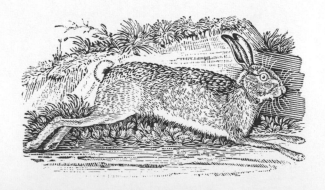

Saddle of Hare with Grape and Brandy Sauce

Priory Hotel, Bath
Chef Mike Collom

Serves 6

6 saddles of hare
4 oz. (125g.) white grapes
4 oz. (125g.) black grapes
1 pint (570ml.) veal stock
2 fl. oz. (50ml.) brandy
1 tablespoon Madeira
4 oz. (125g.) butter
1 small bunch watercress
Worcestershire sauce

Remove the skin and any sinew from the saddle. Season with salt and pepper and seal very quickly in a hot frying pan. Remove and place in a roasting tray and pop in a hot oven for 10 to 15 minutes – the hare should remain pink to avoid being dry.

Whilst roasting, cut the grapes in half and remove the pips. Marinade in the brandy.

Take the cooked saddles from the roasting tin and remove the fillets. Keep warm. Chop up some of the bones for use in the sauce.

Add the veal stock and chopped up bones, the Madeira and the brandy which has been marinading the grapes, to the cooking juices in the tin. Reduce by half and strain into a clean pan.

Add half the grapes, a dash of Worcester sauce and finish with butter until the sauce is of a syrupy consistency.

Slice the warm fillets of hare lengthwise and arrange neatly on hot plates. Decorate each plate with the black and white grapes and pour over the sauce. Garnish with a sprig of watercress.

Fillet of Hare Saddle with Morels

Rogers, Windermere
Chef/proprietor Roger Pergl-Wilson

Serves 2

1 hare saddle boned (keep
  bones for the stock)
4–6 dried Morels (soaked until
  soft)
½ teaspoon of Dijon mustard
1 tablespoon of sherry vinegar
2 tablespoons of Madeira
1 oz. (25g.) butter
1 tablespoon oil
2 tablespoons cream
a little chopped parsley

Bone the saddle and make a good stock with the bones.
Reduce to 3–4 tablespoons.

Melt the butter and oil in a frying pan. Season the fillets and
seal them, browning a little. Cover and cook for a few
minutes. Be sure to keep them under cooked. Remove and
keep warm.

De-glaze the pan with the sherry vinegar, add the mustard,
stock, morells and Madeira. Reduce to a light coating
consistency.

Slice the fillets on the diagonal into about 8 pieces and lay
it out on a plate. Surround or coat with the sauce. Sprinkle
with the parsley.

Hasen Rucken Peter Kaiser

Stane Street Hollow, Pulborough
Chef/proprietor Rene Kaiser

Serves 2

1 saddle of hare
2 oz. (50g.) bacon, chopped
3½ oz. (100g.) mushrooms,
   sliced
2 dessertspoons brandy
3½ fl. oz. (100ml.) game stock
3½ fl. oz. (100ml.) double cream
salt and black pepper
one apple peeled, cut in half,
   decored and poached
a little redcurrant jelly or
   cranberries to fill apple halves

Well trim the saddle of hare and seal in a frying pan. Roast in an oven at 450F/230C/Gas 8 for 15 to 20 minutes. Tip off the excess fat and keep saddle in a warm place.

In a pan put the bacon and the sliced mushrooms, flame with the brandy, add the game stock and the double cream. Boil for 2 minutes.

Loosen the fillets from the saddle and slice. Return to the carcass arranging neatly.

To serve pour the sauce over the saddle of hare and garnish with an apple half filled with cranberries or redcurrant jelly.

Jugged Hare

Fox & Goose, Fressingfield
Chef/proprietor A. P. Clarke

1 hare, jointed, 2 forelegs, 2
   hindlegs, 3 back portions
2 medium onions, thinly sliced
4 large carrots, thinly sliced
4 sticks of celery, thinly sliced
1 small head of fennel, thinly
   sliced
4 cloves garlic, finely chopped
2 bouquet garni
4 rashers of streaky bacon,
   sliced
4 oz. (125g.) butter
2 tablespoons of olive oil
2 tablespoons of flour
1 pint (570ml.) beef stock
1 pint (570ml.) red wine
½ pint (275ml.) port
water as needed

Remember that a large part of the cooking of this dish is done the day before!

Melt the butter and oil. Gently fry the bacon until brown and place in a large casserole. Fry all the vegetables until slightly soft and place them on top of the bacon. In the remaining fat fry the pieces of hare until sealed and just turning brown, place on top of the vegetables and bacon.

With the remaining fat (if there's not enough add a little more butter) make a roux with the flour. Add the wine, port and stock and bring to a rapid boil. Pour this sauce over the hare and vegetables, season with a little salt and black pepper and cook for about two hours in a preheated oven 350F/180C/Gas 4. Allow to cool and refrigerate overnight.

Next day take all the fat off the surface of the casserole and remove the pieces of hare. Bring the remaining stock back to the boil (add a few mushrooms if required) and flame with cognac. Return the pieces of hare to the pot and cook for a further hour in a preheated oven 350F/180C/Gas 4.

You may like to serve this deliciously rich dish with some thyme and lemon forcemeat balls and redcurrant jelly.

Jugged Hare

Tyrrells, Oundle
Chef Sara Jenson

1 hare, jointed
1 bouquet garni
4 rashers bacon
2 pints (900ml.) good meat stock
2 teaspoons redcurrant jelly
1 glass of port
1½ tablespoons flour
1 onion stuck with 10 cloves
6 bay leaves
1 teaspoon mace
salt and black pepper

For the forcemeat balls:

1 hare heart
1 hare liver
1 hare kidney
stock
1 teaspoon thyme
2 tablespoons parsley, chopped
juice and rind one lemon
2 beaten eggs
2 oz. (50g.) suet
4 oz. (125g.) soft breadcrumbs
salt and pepper

Flour the hare and fry in butter.

Put the hare into a large casserole with the chopped bacon. Add the flour blended with the stock. Add onion and seasonings, cover and simmer at 350F/180C/Gas 4 until tender – about 3 hours.

Remove the onion. Add the redcurrant jelly and port. Re-heat without boiling. Serve with forcemeat balls just put in for the last few minutes to heat through.

To make the forcemeat balls cook the heart, liver and kidneys in a little stock for 3 minutes. Remove from stock and chop very finely. Mix with the thyme, parsley, lemon rind and juice, suet, salt and pepper. Roll into small balls and dip into the beaten egg and coat in soft breadcrumbs. Fry in butter till brown.

Terrine of Rabbit with Pork and Prunes

Homewood Park, Hinton Charterhouse
Chef/proprietor Stephen Ross

Serves 8–10

1 wild rabbit
1 lb. (450g.) belly pork
8 oz. (225g.) smokey bacon
4 oz. (125g.) prunes, stoned
   and soaked in brandy
salt and pepper
½ clove garlic, finely chopped
½ small onion, finely chopped
½ oz. (15g.) juniper berries
1 egg
pickled fruits or chutney to
   accompany

Remove the saddlemeat from the rabbit in two strips and set aside.

Mince the legmeat with the pork and bacon in a fine mincer. Mix in the remaining ingredients except for the prunes.

Put a third of the mixture in the bottom of a terrine. Lay half of the saddlemeat lengthways down the terrine with a layer of prunes between the two strips of meat. The next third of the mixture on top and repeat the process using up all the mixture. Cook in a bain-marie for 1 hour in a low oven.

Allow to cool with a light weight over the terrine. Do not discard the juices surrounding the terrine which will set as a delicious jelly. When cold turn out, slice and serve with pickled fruits or chutneys.

Rabbit Pâté with Beer

Tyrrells, Oundle
Chef Sara Jenson

2 lbs. (900g.) rabbit, boned
   and chopped
½ pint (275ml.) light ale
1 lb. (450g.) pork belly skinned
   and chopped
salt and pepper
thyme
parsley
2 bay leaves
bacon rasher

Put the boned chopped rabbit in a bowl with the light ale, the chopped pork belly, a little salt, pepper, thyme and parsley. Add two bay leaves, and leave to soak overnight.

Remove the meat from the marinade and mince the pork and rabbit separately.

Line a fire-proof dish with bacon rashers, pack layers of minced rabbit and pork on top, pour the beer liquid over. Bake for 2½–3 hours in a slow oven. Serve with crusty bread.

Wild Rabbit Set in an Apple and Juniper Jelly

Popjoys, Bath
Chef/proprietor Ali Golden

Serves 8

2 wild rabbits, skinned, gutted
  and cut into quarters
bouquet garni
1 onion, chopped
1 carrot, chopped
cup of white wine
1 pint (570ml.) chicken stock
1 pint (570ml.) apple juice
2 oz. (50g.) juniper berries
gelatine for setting
few thyme flowers or herbs for
  decoration

This excellent recipe can be easily varied by adding different herbs or green peppercorns to the jelly.

Put the rabbit in a casserole with the bouquet garni, onion, carrots, cup of white wine and the chicken stock. Simmer the rabbit until tender but not dried out – pressure cookers can be useful here.

Take the meat off the bone and reserve.

Return the bones to the stock in the casserole and reduce the liquid until you have ½ pint (275ml.). Add the apple juice and crushed juniper berries and simmer for 10 minutes to infuse the flavours. Strain into a measuring jug. Measure the liquid and add the requisite amount of gelatine to make a jelly.

Line ramekins with clingfilm to overlap the edges. Pour a little of the liquid jelly into the bottoms of the ramekins and allow to set.

Pile the rabbit bits, cut into neat hunks, onto the set jelly base and fill with the remaining liquid jelly. Decorate the tops with thyme flowers or other herb flowers before the jelly has quite set so that they stay in place.

When the jellies are well set, pull the clingfilm out of the ramekins and unmould the jellies. Serve on white plates with homemade chutnies or a crispy apple and walnut salad.

78

Ballantine de Lapin Truffée au Queues de Langoustines

Longueville Manor, Jersey
Chef John Dicken

1 rabbit
1½ lbs. (700g.) rabbit leg meat
12 oz. (350g.) pork shoulder
11 oz. (300g.) back fat
2 fl. oz. (50ml.) Armagnac
1 shallot
½ oz. (15g.) butter
¼ clove garlic
1 sprig thyme
1 teaspoon marjoram or
  tarragon
3 teaspoons parsley
1 oz. (25g.) salt
⅓ oz. (10g.) pepper
pinch of salt and pepper
18 fl. oz. (500ml.) rabbit stock
4 large Dublin Bay prawn tails
4 large leaves of spinach

Line a 10" (25cm.) terrine with the back fat.

Dissect the rabbit, keeping the loin whole and boning out the legs.

Marinate the rabbit meat, pork shoulder, and back fat in the Armagnac, seasoning, chopped shallots and garlic for 24 hours.

Prepare the white rabbit stock with the carcass.

Wrap the loin and cooked Dublin Bay prawns in the blanched leaves of spinach.

Pass the marinated ingredients through a fine mincer into a bowl. Add the finely chopped herbs and the cold jellied stock.

Fill the terrine arranging the garnish through the middle. Cook in a bain-marie at 375F/190C/Gas 5 for 45–55 minutes.

Paupiettes of Wild Rabbit with Lovage and Mustard

Croque-en-bouche, Malvern Wells
Chefs/proprietors Robin and Marion Jones

Serves 6

3 young wild rabbits
salt and pepper
¾ pint (400ml.) light stock
2 tablespoons of Dijon mustard
2 tablespoons of calvados

For the stuffing:

1 small onion, finely chopped
1 clove garlic, finely chopped
1½ oz. (40g.) butter
1 heaped tablespoon
   breadcrumbs
1 egg yolk
6 young lovage stems about 8″
   (20.5cm.) high

For the marinade:

2 tablespoons of white wine
4 tablespoons of olive oil
juice of 1 lemon

Much of the preparation for this dish should be carried out the day before you wish to eat it.

The day before cooking, separate the haunches of rabbit by cutting just behind the shoulders. Cut down each side of the backbone and separate back legs from the carcass. Bone out each back leg. Mix the marinade ingredients and pour over the rabbit. Turn occasionally. Use the shoulder and other bones to make a light stock.

For the stuffing, cook the onion and garlic in butter till soft. Mix with crumbs and seasoning. When cool add the egg yolk and chopped lovage leaves. (Chop the stalks and leave them till later).

To cook, drain the rabbit pieces on kitchen paper. Spread out each boneless haunch and coat lightly inside with half of the mustard. Divide stuffing between six pieces and fold each over to make small parcels. Tie these with string.

Heat a large flameproof dish on the stove, brush with oil, add the butter and quickly brown the rabbit parcels, turning them with two wooden spoons. Pull the dish off the heat, season with salt and black pepper, flame with calvados, pour on stock and add the chopped lovage stalks. Lift the parcels onto a rack across the dish. Put into a hot oven 425F/220C/Gas 7, cooking 10 minutes each side and basting at least twice.

When cooked, put in a warm place to rest while making the sauce.

Strain the cooking juices into a small pan, scraping out the bottom with a little water if necessary. Add the cream and the remaining mustard and reduce to a good consistency.

To serve, remove the string and cut each parcel into 5 or 6 small slices. Arrange on a large dish. Pour the sauce over or around and garnish with some more lovage leaves.

Wild Rabbit in White Wine and Mustard

Flowers, Bath
Chef/proprietor Teresa Lipin

Serves 4–6

2 small wild rabbits, jointed
1 large onion, roughly chopped
1 clove garlic, crushed
1 stick celery, roughly chopped
bouquet garni
1 leek, finely chopped
seasoned flour
1 tablespoon French mustard
1 bottle dry white wine
1 dessertspoon double cream
salt and pepper
pinch thyme
croutons, to garnish
parsley, to garnish

Heat some oil and sauté the vegetables and garlic. Put in a casserole.

Roll the rabbit pieces in the seasoned flour and fry until sealed. Add to the casserole.

Deglaze the pan with a cupful of wine and add to the casserole. Add a bouquet garni, salt and pepper. Place the casserole in a moderate oven and cook for about 30 minutes.

To serve, remove the rabbit pieces from the casserole and reduce the sauce. Stir in the cream and garnish with croutons and parsley.

Rabbit with Prune Purée

The Count House, Botallack
Chef Celia Reynolds

1 rabbit, skinned and trimmed
½ lb. (225g.) prunes
1 tablespoon oil
1 tablespoon butter
1 teaspoon vinegar
½ pint (275ml.) red wine
½ pint (275ml.) chicken stock
1 clove garlic, crushed
bouquet garni
salt and ground black pepper
1 tablespoon parsley, chopped

For the marinade:

5 fl. oz. (150ml.) red wine
large bouquet garni
1 onion, coarsely chopped
1 carrot, coarsely chopped
6 slightly crushed peppercorns
1 tablespoon oil

Divide the skinned and trimmed rabbit into six portions. Place into a bowl, add the marinade ingredients, pouring over the oil last. Leave at room temperature turning occasionally, for 4–12 hours.

Drain the rabbit, pat dry with a paper towel. Strain the marinade, reserve the vegetables and liquid.

Heat the oil and butter in a shallow casserole, and brown the rabbit on all sides. Remove from pan. Add the onion and carrot from the marinade and sauté slightly until soft. Add the vinegar and liquid from the marinade and the red wine. Bring to the boil. Add the stock, garlic, bouquet garni and seasoning, return the rabbit dishes to the pan. Drain the prunes, and add to the pan. Cover and simmer for 35–45 minutes until the rabbit is tender. Remove the rabbit and prunes and strain the sauce into another pan. Skim the fat.

Stone and purée one third of the prunes in a blender. Reheat the sauce and whisk in the purée. Reduce to a thin coating consistency. Transfer the rabbit to a serving dish, and spoon over the prunes. Pour over the sauce and sprinkle with parsley just before serving.

Rabbit in Potacchio

Walnut Tree, Llandewi Skirrid
Chef/proprietor Franco Taruschio

1 wild rabbit, chopped and
  thoroughly washed
white wine vinegar
olive oil
garlics, unpeeled but slightly
  crushed
dry white wine
few sprigs rosemary
salt and pepper
stock

This dish originates from the Marche region in the central east coast of Italy.

Put the rabbit to soak in water and a little white wine vinegar for half a day or until the meat is white.

Drain the pieces of rabbit and dry well. Season and fry in olive oil until lightly browned. Add the garlics, white wine and a few sprigs of parsley. Cover and cook until the meat is tender. Remove the rabbit from the juices and reduce and check seasoning. Serve the sauce, garlics and rosemary over and around the rabbit pieces. Some stock can be added to the juices to intensify the flavour of the sauce.

Venison

July – February

Escalopes of Venison with Yoghurt and Chive Sauce

Homewood Park, Hinton Charterhouse
Chef/proprietor Stephen Ross

Serves 6

Ask your butcher to prepare 2 escalopes per person (about 3–4 oz./75–125g. each) from the haunch of a roe deer – loin may be used but is much more extravagant

For the sauce:

½ pint (275ml.) concentrated chicken stock
¼ bottle dry white wine
5 fl. oz. (150ml.) double cream
5 fl. oz. (150ml.) plain yoghurt
fresh chives, chopped
rind and juice of 1 lemon
salt and pepper

Quickly sauté the escalopes in hot butter, colouring the meat but not cooking beyond pink in the middle. Keep warm and retain any juices.

In the same pan add the white wine and chicken stock and reduce by half. Add the cream, bring to the boil, season and add the chives, lemon juice and rind. Remove from the heat, add the yoghurt and serve immediately. Do not boil again after adding the yoghurt.

Loin of Venison with Fresh Damson and Juniper Sauce

Woods, Bath
Chef Mary Alley

Serves 2

1 loin of venison, middle of the
best end
10 juniper berries, crushed
¾ pint (400ml.) reduced veal
stock
2 shallots, finely sliced
5 fl. oz. (150ml.) red wine
vinegar
2 oz. (50g.) fresh damsons,
stoned
grated rind of an orange and
lemon
1 tablespoon of damson jam
1 tablespoon of dripping (from
veal and venison bones)
1 oz. (25g.) butter
½ pint (275ml.) red wine

To make the sauce base, fry the shallots in melted butter for about 2 minutes until transparent. Add the vinegar, veal stock, wine, jam and grated rind. Reduce until left with approximately half a pint (275ml.) of liquid.

Season the venison with salt and pepper and crushed juniper berries. Heat the dripping until almost smoking, and place venison in pan. Seal on all sides. Cook under a pre-heated grill for 10–12 minutes. Remove from pan and leave to rest. Pour off the fat from the pan, add the sauce and bring up to the boil.

Add the fresh damsons and heat through. Adjust seasoning to taste. To serve carve the venison and arrange on a plate, and pour the sauce over.

Medallions of Venison with Blackcurrant Pepper Glaze

Marlfield House, Gorey
Chef/proprietor Mary Bowe

Serves 4

2 fillets of venison, cut into
   medallions
4 oz. (125g.) blackcurrants
crushed black and green
   peppercorns
1 pint (570ml.) venison stock
half spoon honey
blackcurrant vinegar, if available
butter
salt and black pepper

Sweat off the crushed peppercorns and onions in a little butter, add the blackcurrant and venison stock and a little blackcurrant vinegar. Simmer for 20 minutes. Pass through a fine chinoise and season. Keep warm.

Allow 3 small medallions of venison per person. Season with salt and mill over black pepper before cooking. Pan fry in a little hot oil.

Place the pan fried medallions on a baking tray when cooked and brush a little honey on each. Glaze underneath the grill for 2 minutes.

Place the sauce on the base of the plate, put the medallions on top and garnish.

Medallions of Venison with Pears and Cinnamon

Rogers, Windermere
Chef/proprietor Roger Pergl-Wilson

Serves 4

2 lbs. (900g.) loin of venison, trimmed of all fat, and cut into 8 or 12 medallions of ½" (1cm.) thick
2 good sized pears
1" (2.5cm.) stick of cinnamon ground in a coffee grinder
1 dessertspoon of blackcurrant jelly
1 tablespoon of red wine vinegar
2 oz. (50g.) butter
2 tablespoons oil
4 tablespoons port
5 fl. oz. (150ml.) good venison stock

Peel the pears and using a small parisienne cutter, cut into little balls slightly larger than pea size – alternatively you could just dice them if you have no cutter. Keep in slightly salted water until needed.

Brown the venison off quickly in the oil and butter. Season. Remove from the pan and keep warm.

Sauté the pears until lightly brown and remove.

Add the jelly and vinegar to the pan and work together and reduce until sticky. Add the stock. Sprinkle the cinnamon over the pears and add to the sauce, cook through until a good coating consistency is reached. Pour around or over the venison.

Medallion de Chevreuil Sauce Grand-Veneur

Ortolan, Shinfield
Chef/proprietor J. W. Burton-Race

saddle of venison, bones
    retained, cut into medallions

For the marinade:

mirepoix of celery, 6 leeks, 3
    onions, 3 carrots
little thyme
bay leaf
garlic
crushed black peppercorns
5 juniper berries, crushed
2 pieces orange rind

For the sauce:

2 tablespoons redcurrant jelly
7 fl. oz. (200ml.) white wine
    vinegar
11 fl. oz. (300ml.) port
1 ladle glace de viande (meat
    glaze)
1 tablespoon caster sugar
3½ fl. oz. (100ml.) Madeira
14 fl. oz. (400ml.) white wine
1¾ pints (1 litre) chicken stock
armagnac

Place the venison in the dry marinade and marinate for a couple of days.

Roast the finely chopped bones in a hot oven, sprinkle with flour and singe. When nicely browned, remove from oven.

Meanwhile fry the mirepoix from the marinade until soft and golden brown.

In a large flat bottomed pan, caramelise the sugar and the jelly and cook out. Add the bones and stir constantly until well coated and sticky. Add the vinegar and reduce until dry with no acid smell. Add the Madeira and reduce until dry. Add the port and reduce by half. Add the mirepoix and cover the bones with stock. Bring to the boil, skim gently and simmer for 1½ hours. Pass through a fine chinois. Skim and reduce by half, finishing with the glace de viande.

Cook the venison in a heavy bottom pan. Remove and flame the pan with armagnac. Add the sauce base, correct seasoning and finish with a little butter. Pour around the medallions of venison.

Pan Fried Venison with a Fruity Sauce

Pool Court, Pool-in-Wharfedale
Chef Melvin Jordan

Serves 6–8

loin or fillet of venison, cut into
    rounds ½" (1.5cm.) thick
½ medium onion, finely
    chopped
1 orange, juiced and zested
1 lemon, juiced and zested
½ pint (275ml.) ruby port
1 dessertspoon English
    mustard
½ oz. (15g.) butter
1 tablespoon arrowroot diluted
    with 2 tablespoons cold water
salt and pepper

Blanch the orange and lemon zest in boiling water to
remove any bitterness. Melt the butter and sweat the onion.
Add port and bring to the boil – flame and allow to burn
itself out. Add the jelly, mustard, orange and lemon juice.
Bring back to the boil and thicken with arrowroot. Lastly,
add orange and lemon zest and season to taste. This sauce
may also be served cold with a game terrine.

Trim the fillet or loin of any sinew and marinate if desired.
Fry in a little butter on both sides until pink in the middle.
Serve suitably garnished and offer the sauce separately.

Noisettes of Venison with Marc de Bourgogne

Gidleigh Park, Chagford
Chef Shaun Hill

Serves 4

4 lb. (1.8kg.) saddle of venison
8 oz. (225g.) mirepoix of
  vegetables (carrots, celery,
  onion, cut into small dice)
5 fl. oz. (150ml.) game or veal
  stock
2 fl. oz. (50ml.) marc de
  Bourgogne
1 fl. oz. (25ml.) Sauternes
3 oz. (75g.) unsalted butter

Cut the noisettes from the saddle, season and reserve.

Chop the bones and colour in a frying pan with the mirepoix of vegetables. Add the stock and simmer for 30 minutes only. Strain and then reduce by half. Whisk in the butter, piece by piece until the sauce thickens. Add the Sauternes and the marc de Bourgogne.

Sauté the reserved noisettes and coat with the sauce.

Venison with Thyme

Michaels, Bristol
Chef/proprietor Michael McGowan

good pieces venison (preferably
   roe-deer), approximately ½″
   (1 cm.) thick
fresh thyme, chopped
white wine
butter
oil
salt and black papper

For Francatelli's venison sauce:

2 tablespoons port
8 oz. (225g.) redcurrant jelly
1 stick cinnamon
pared rind of 1 lemon

Trim any fat or sinews from the meat. Brush with oil and sprinkle with salt and black pepper.

Take a large thick bottom frying pan and heat some butter until foaming. Fry the pieces of venison for about 2 minutes on each side, adding the fresh thyme towards the end of the cooking. Cover the pan and leave off the heat for a few minutes to allow the meat to relax.

Take the meat out of the pan and place on hot plates. Add some white wine to the pan to deglaze and pour the resulting liquid over the meat. Serve with sautéed potatoes, a salad and Francatelli's venison sauce served separately.

Make the venison sauce by placing all the ingredients into a sauce pan and bringing to the boil. Simmer for 10 minutes, strain and serve.

Marinated Saddle of Venison with Celeriac Purée

Sharrow Bay, Ullswater
Chefs Juan Martin and Colin Akrigg

1 small saddle of venison
8 spinach leaves

For the marinade:
mirepoix of carrot, celery, onion
 and garlic
2 bay leaves
1 sprig fresh thyme
8 black peppercorns
6 juniper berries
½ pint (275ml.) red wine

For the sauce:
¼ pint (150ml.) good beef stock
 (or demi-glace if available)
½ pint (275ml.) good brown
 venison stock
1 tablespoon redcurrant jelly
2 tablespoons port

For the purée:
½ lb. (225g.) celeriac
2 eggs
½ pint (275ml.) double cream
salt and pepper

Bone and trim the venison. Place in the marinade and leave for 24 hours.

To make the sauce, add the marinade, stock, beef stock, redcurrant jelly together in a large pan and reduce to desired consistency. Finish with port and seasoning.

Prepare the celeriac and cut into fine dice. Sweat in butter until soft. Add the double cream and reduce until most of the cream has been absorbed, then liquidise with the eggs and seasoning. Pour into buttered dariole moulds and steam gently for about 20 minutes.

To serve, cut the venison into desired portions and cook in a very hot oven for 4–5 minutes. Dip spinach leaves into hot fat for a few seconds to soften, then cover each plate with the leaves. Turn out the dariole of celeriac and place in the centre of the plate. Slice venison and fan around the celeriac moulds and coat lightly with the sauce.

Fillet of Roe Deer with Caraway Seed Pancakes

Morels, Haslemere
Chef/proprietor J. Morel

1 saddle of roe deer, boned
  and cut into 10 portions
  (retain bones for stock)
2 onions, washed and chopped,
  not peeled
3 carrots, washed and
  chopped, not peeled
1 stick of celery, washed and
  chopped
bouquet garni
1 teaspoon juniper berries
1 tablespoon coriander seeds
1 teaspoon black peppercorns
3 cloves garlic, crushed
1 pint (570ml.) good veal stock
1 glass of port
1 bottle of good Rhone wine
knob of butter

For the pancakes:

1 pint (570ml.) pancake butter
1 tablespoon caraway seeds
½ oz. (15g.) yeast

Make the pancakes in advance. Add a tablespoon of caraway seeds to the batter and add the yeast. Leave to rise and then cook the pancakes in small pans – a blini pan is good for this but if this cannot be obtained, use a very small frying pan.

Make a stock by chopping the bones from the carcass and browning in a hot oven. Place the bones in a large pot, add the vegetables, the juniper berries, coriander seeds, peppercorns and garlic. Cover with water and cook gently for 4 hours. Strain the stock and reduce by half by cooking with the lid off.

Pour the wine into a saucepan and cook for 10 minutes. Add the veal stock and game stock to the wine and cook with the lid off until reduced and syrupy. Put aside.

Sauté the fillets of roe deer for 4 minutes in a hot pan (they should be very pink). Slice the fillets and arrange on a serving dish. Keep warm. Warm the sauce, adding the glass of port. Pour the sauce around the fillets. Serve the pancakes separately or arranged on top of the fillets.

Chicken Breast Stuffed with Venison Mousse

French Partridge, Horton
Chef/proprietor David Partridge

6 chicken breasts with wing
  bones
4 oz. (125g.) well trimmed lean
  venison
3 fl. oz. (75ml.) cream (40%)
1 oz. (25g.) venison glaze (or
  other concentrated stock)
1 egg
butter for frying
salt and pepper
sage, thyme and parsley

For the sauce:

sherry glass cognac
game stock
8 fl. oz. (225ml.) cream (40%)

Skin the chicken breasts and trim meat from wing bone.
Fold out fillet and flatten out.

Prepare the mousse by chopping the venison in a food
processor. Add the raw egg and seasoning to taste. When
smooth add the cream and glaze.

Insert a boning knife at the thick end of the chicken breast
and slit along, working to make a pocket. Fill a forcing bag
with venison mousse and pipe carefully into each chicken
breast.

Melt the butter in a low sided saucepan and gently fry the
chicken, pocket side down first. Season with salt and
pepper.

De-glaze the pan with the cognac and stock. Cover the pan
and allow to steam gently for about 4 minutes. Do not over
cook.

Remove the chicken to a warm place and finish the sauce
by adding cream to the pan juices. Reduce and adjust
seasoning.

Venison and Steak Pie

Bistro Twenty One, Bristol
Chef/proprietor Stephen Markwick

Serves 6–8

3 lb. (1.25 kilos) shoulder
  venison
1 lb. (450g.) good stewing steak
½ lb. (225g.) streaky bacon, cut
  into lardons
4 oz. (125g.) button onions
4 oz. (125g.) mushrooms
good stock
tomato purée
1 lb. (450g.) shortcrust pastry

For the marinade:

½ pint (275ml.) red wine
2 fl. oz. (50ml.) olive oil
2 fl. oz. (50ml.) red wine vinegar
1 onion, chopped
4 garlics, chopped
thyme
6–9 juniper berries, crushed

This pie can be made even better with the addition of further game, such as hare or pheasant. The marinade ingredients are really a guide and can easily be added to with anything that you fancy.

Cut and trim the venison and beef into good size pieces and marinade for at least 1 day – it will keep in the marinade for much longer.

Drain meat and seal well in a very hot frying pan. Put into casserole. Fry the vegetables from the marinade and add. Add a little flour and some tomato purée, also the juices from the marinade, stock and possibly some more red wine. Bring to the boil, check seasoning and simmer, covered, in a cool oven for 1–1½ hours.

Toss the streaky bacon, button onions and mushrooms in frying pan and add to the casserole about 20–25 minutes before the end of cooking.

When the casserole is done, leave to cool and put into a pie dish. Cover with the pastry and bake in a hot oven for about 30 minutes.

Game Fish

Caveached Salmon

Thornbury Castle, Thornbury
Chef Kenneth Bell

1½ lb. (675g.) centre cut of
   salmon

For the marinade:

6 fl. oz. (175ml.) dry white wine
1 tablespoon salt
¼ teaspoon ground pepper
juice 1 lemon
juice 1 orange
¼ onion, finely chopped
1 clove garlic, finely chopped
2 fl. oz. (50ml.) very best oil

Cut the salmon horizontally in half and trim completely of skin and bone, leaving two fillets weighing probably ½ lb. (225g.) each. Cut each into three little steaks, each portion should weigh between 2–3 oz. (50–75g.)

Mix together all the ingredients for the marinade and pour over the salmon pieces. Put into the refrigerator. Shake the container occasionally to ensure the marinade is in contact with all sides of the salmon fillets.

The salmon can be eaten after 6 hours in the marinade but is at its best at 24 to 48 hours. Serve as a first course, decorated with a little salad.

Petite Roulade de Saumon

Priory Hotel, Bath
Chef Mike Collom

Serves 6

1 lb. (450g.) salmon
1 pint (570ml.) double cream
cayenne pepper
3 egg whites
½ teaspoon salt
2 teaspoons tarragon, chopped
12 oz. (350g.) puff pastry

For the sauce:

1 pint (570ml.) fish stock
1 tablespoon shallots, chopped
knob of butter
5 fl. oz. (150ml.) whipping
   cream
1 teaspoon tarragon, chopped

Remove all the skin and any bones from the salmon and place in a blender with the egg whites. Blend and pass the salmon mixture through a sieve.

Add salt and mix well with a wooden spoon till the salmon becomes firm and slightly rubbery.

Place the bowl containing the salmon mixture on a bed of crushed ice and slowly beat in the double cream. Add the cayenne and set aside.

Roll out the puff pastry, approx. 12" (30.5cm.) long by 5" (12.5cm.) wide, and brush egg wash around the edge. Using a spoon and palette knife, arrange the mixture 1" (2.5cm.) in from the edge. Sprinkle a little tarragon on the salmon and seal both ends.

Place on a baking sheet, brush with egg wash and decorate with strips of puff pastry. Allow to rest for 30 minutes refrigerated.

Bake in an oven 420F/220C/Gas 7 for 15–20 minutes or until the pastry is crisp and golden. Remove from the oven and rest for 5 minutes before slicing.

To make the sauce, take the fish stock and the shallots and boil down to reduce by half. Add the whipping cream and the chopped tarragon. Reduce the sauce in a shallow pan until it coats the back of a spoon. Add a knob of butter whisking it in till smooth. Serve with the roulade.

Escalope of Wild Salmon with Red Onions and Shredded Lettuce

Woods, Bicester
Chef/proprietor Robert Harrison

Serves 4

4 escalopes salmon, 6 oz.
  (175g.) each
olive oil
sea salt
2 red onions, finely chopped
1 tablespoon white wine
  vinegar
1 tablespoon water
1 glass dry white wine
1 tablespoon lemon juice
1 teaspoon whipping cream
7 oz. (200g.) unsalted butter
¼ small web or iceberg lettuce,
  shredded
herb of your choice

Sweat the onions in a little of the butter. Add the vinegar, water and wine and reduce by ⅔. Incorporate the cream, whisk in the butter and finally the lettuce. Cook very gently for a few moments.

Brush the salmon with oil and season. Grill over hot charcoal. Arrange on a plate and pour over the sauce.

Darne de Saumon aux Pointes d'Asperges

Mallory Court, Bishops Tachbrook
Chef/proprietor Allan Holland

4 middle cut steaks of wild
　　salmon
20 spears of asparagus
fish stock or water
lemon, to garnish
sprigs of chervil to garnish

For the mousseline:

6 sole fillets
½ egg white
7 fl. oz. (200ml.) double cream
salt and pepper

Prepare the salmon steaks, season with white pepper and salt and put aside.

For the mousseline, grease 4 small castle moulds. Purée the fish fillets and rub through a fine sieve. Mix in the egg white and place in a bowl over ice. Beat in the double cream very slowly, mixing well until you have a light fluffy mousse. Season to taste with salt. Fill the moulds with the mixture and place in a tray half filled with boiling water. Lay a piece of foil over the top and poach in a low oven 300F/150C/Gas 2 for about 15 minutes or until firm.

For the sauce, put two tablespoons of water with the crushed peppercorns and white wine vinegar into a small pan and reduce by two thirds. Take the pan off the heat and put in 1 tablespoon of water and the egg yolks whisking continuously. Place the pan over a very gentle heat and continue whisking the egg mixture until it becomes creamy. Remove from the heat and begin whisking in the melted butter slowly. Add the lemon, season to taste. Fold in the lightly whipped cream.

For the sauce:

3 egg yolks

9 oz. (250g.) melted butter

juice of 1 lemon

1 tablespoon white wine
vinegar

1 teaspoon white peppercorns,
crushed

5 oz. (150g.) double cream,
lightly whipped

Bring a steamer filled with fish stock or water to simmering point. Place the salmon steaks and asparagus tips into the steamer and cover and steam for about 10 minutes or until the salmon and asparagus are cooked. Remove the skin and bone from the salmon and divide the steaks into 2 halves. Arrange the two halves of the steak to form a fan shape on the plate. Place the mousseline in the centre and arrange the asparagus tips around the top edge of the plate. Coat the mousseline with some of the sauce and garnish with a slice of lemon and a sprig of chervil.

Wild Salmon in Saffron Sauce

The Old Monastery, Drybridge
Chef/proprietor Douglas Craig

Serves 4

1½ lb. (700g.) wild salmon fillets
   (or sea trout), gutted,
   beheaded and filleted
8 spring onions, chopped
½ oz. (15g.) butter
4 fl. oz. (125ml.) good fish stock
4 fl. oz. (125ml.) dry vermouth
8 fl. oz. (225ml.) double cream
1 sachet saffron
salt and black pepper
1 teaspoon fresh dill, chopped

Remove the skin and flesh from the fish and cut into slices ½" (1cm.) thick.

Sweat the spring onions in the butter without colouring in a shallow pan. Add the vermouth and bring to the boil. Place the fish in the liquor and return to the simmer. Cover and cook for 3–4 minutes.

Place the fish on a heated serving dish and keep warm. Add the fish stock to the cooking liquor and reduce. Add the cream and saffron and reduce still further. Season to taste, add the dill and pour over the fish.

Braised Salmon with Pike Mousse

Gravetye Manor, East Grinstead
Chef Allan Garth

Serves 4

4 x 4oz. (125g.) pieces of
   salmon fillet
18 fl. oz. (500ml.) fish stock, for
   braising
chives, to decorate

For the pike mousse:

9 oz. (250g.) pike, without skin
   and bones
11 fl. oz. (300ml.) double cream
1 whole egg
salt and pepper

For the sauce:

3½ fl. oz. (100ml.) fish stock
3½ fl. oz. (100ml.) white wine
7 fl. oz. (200ml.) double cream
2 shallots, chopped
1oz. (25g.) white mushrooms,
   sliced
3 tomatoes, chopped
salt and pepper

Mince the pike flesh twice through a mincer. Season and add the egg. Press the mixture through a sieve.

Place the pike mixture in a bowl on ice and slowly add the double cream with a wooden spoon. Spread the mousse over the fillets of salmon and smooth with a pallet knife. Place the pieces of salmon in a buttered ovenproof dish with the fish and braise in a hot oven for 15 minutes. Finish by glazing under the grill.

To make the sauce, reduce the fish stock and white wine with the tomatoes, shallots and white mushrooms until half the volume. Add the cream and reduce until the right consistency is obtained. Season.

To serve place the braised salmon on the sauce and sprinkle with chopped chives.

Sole Mousse in Scottish Smoked Salmon

The Count House, Botallack
Chef Celia Reynolds

Serves 6

1½ lbs. (700g.) sole, boned and
  skinned
½ lb. (225g.) smoked salmon
2 tomatoes, skinned and
  seeded
1 avocado pear, skinned
1 clove garlic, crushed
4 tablespoons tartare sauce
1 oz. (25g.) gelatine
5 fl. oz. (150ml.) water
1 pint (570ml.) double cream
large prawns to decorate

Grill the sole. Place in food processor.

Melt the gelatine and water in a double pan. When melted add tartare sauce and double cream. Mix with the sole, check seasoning, and chill.

Divide the mousse into three equal parts. Place one third into an oiled mould and return to fridge. Into another third beat the processed tomatoes and 2 oz. (50g.) of smoked salmon. Add to the mould and chill. Into the last third add the processed avocado and crushed garlic. Add to the mould and leave to set overnight.

Turn out from mould, cover with strips of remaining salmon and decorate with prawns, lemon twists and parsley.

Steamed Salmon Trout with a Tomato and Basil Vinaigrette

Restaurant Seventy Four, Canterbury
Chef/proprietor I. L. McAndrew

Serves 6

1 x 1½ lb. (700g.) salmon trout
3 tomatoes
18–20 leaves of fresh basil
18 points of asparagus
3 tablespoons of sherry vinegar
3 tablespoons of walnut oil
⅓ head oak leaf lettuce

This is a warm first-course where you should have everything ready in advance leaving only the cooking of the fish and the finishing of the dish until the last minute.

Scale and fillet and skin the salmon trout. Cut each fillet into six pieces slightly at an angle.

Peel the asparagus and tie in bundles of six. Cook in boiling salted water until they still have a little bite. Refresh in iced water.

Blanch the tomatoes. Deseed and cut the flesh into small dices. Tear the leaves of the basil into small pieces. Mix together the oil, sherry vinegar, basil leaves and tomatoes. Season to taste.

To cook, lay the pieces of salmon into a steaming pan and season. Steam for two minutes. While the salmon is cooking gently warm the vinaigrette through to take the chill off it.

Drop the points of asparagus into boiling water for about thirty seconds to reheat. Cut each point of asparagus into two.

To serve, lay three leaves of lettuce onto each plate and place two slices of fish in the centre of each plate. Scatter the asparagus around the fish and spoon the warm dressing over and around.

Pike with Watercress Sauce

Hope End, Ledbury
Chef/proprietor Patricia Hegarty

Serves 6

5 lb. (2.3kg.) pike
1 pint (570ml.) white wine or
   dry cider

For the sauce:

6 tablespoons apple or wine
   vinegar
6 shallots, finely chopped
9 oz. (250g.) butter
3 bunches of watercress

Chop the head and tail off the pike. Wrap in a foil parcel, moistened with the wine or cider, and bake at 375F/190C/Gas 5 in a roasting tin for about 45 minutes or until cooked. Cool. Skin and fillet the fish, extracting as many bones as possible when dividing fillets into required number of portions.

To make the sauce, reduce the vinegar with the shallots and 1 oz. (25g.) butter to about 1 tablespoon or less. Add the cooking liquor and whizz in the liquidiser. Over a very gentle heat, beat in the remaining butter, piece by piece, until the sauce is thickened and is glossy and smooth. Add the watercress, torn into small pieces, at the last moment. To serve, heat the fillets of pike between 2 plates over a steaming pan. Serve with the sauce garnished with a sprig of watercress.

A Mixed Bag of Game

Game Pâté en Croûte

Ston Easton Park, Ston Easton
Chef M. Harrington

shortcrust pastry, to line terrine
1 hare
1 rabbit
1 pheasant
1 wild duck
4 oz. (125g.) venison
1 guinea fowl

For the marinade:

5 fl. oz. (150ml.) brandy
5 fl. oz. (150ml.) red wine

1 large onion, chopped
2 cloves garlic, crushed
1 oz. (25g.) julienne of truffle
½ oz. (15g.) whole pink
    peppercorns
½ oz. (15g.) juniper berries
pinch fresh thyme
8 oz. (225g.) streaky bacon
½ pint (275ml.) double cream
2 eggs
game flavoured jelly, made from
    trimmings and bones

Make the shortcrust pastry and leave for 24 hours.

Remove all the flesh from the game and set aside the saddle of hare and rabbit, plus one breast each of wild duck and pheasant and marinade in red wine.

Mix together the rest of the flesh, plus the sweated onion, garlic, thyme, black pepper and salt. Whizz in processor till smooth. Leave to cool and then pass through a fine sieve and cool again. Add two eggs and the double cream to this mixture and beat well with a wooden spoon. Fold in the truffle and peppercorns.

Line a pâté tin with the pastry and cover with streaky bacon, overlapping the edges. Place a thin layer of the mixture in the bottom of the mould and then alternately put in the saddle and breasts, finishing with the mixture. Fold over the overlapping bacon and put a lid of short pastry on top. Make a line of holes along the length of the pastry to allow the steam to escape. Decorate with pastry leaves and egg wash the top. Cook in the oven at 325F/170C/Gas 3 for 1¼ hours and leave to cool. When the pie is cold fill with a game flavoured jelly made from the trimmings and bones. Serve with a Cumberland sauce.

Terrine of Game

Thornbury Castle, Thornbury
Chef Colin Hingston

Serves 12

1 lb. (450g.) game meat, mixed
  or one type only
8 oz. (225g.) veal
8 oz. (225g.) calf's liver
8 oz. (225g.) calf's kidney
1 teaspoon ground allspice
1 teaspoon ground coriander
2 cloves garlic
2 teaspoons salt
ground black pepper
1 orange, juice and grated zest
4 oz. (125g.) breadcrumbs
1 glass of orange Curacao
streaky bacon to line the terrine
pistachio nuts

Place all the ingredients, apart from the bacon and nuts, into a food processor and whizz to a fine paste. Mix in the pistachio nuts.

Place the mixture into a lined terrine and bake in a bain-marie in a warm oven at 350F/180C/Gas 4 for about 45 minutes. To test that the terrine is ready, stick with a skewer – when the juices run clear it is ready.

Leave to cool pressed under a weight. Leave for 24 hours. Serve the terrine of game with Cumberland Sauce.

The Best of Game

Fischer's, Bakewell
Chef/proprietor Max Fischer

Serves 6

For the venison:

1 lb. (450g.) saddle of venison

1 lb. (450g.) venison bones and
trimmings

mirepoix of vegetabes – onions,
carrots and celery

1 fl. oz. (25ml.) brandy

1 fl. oz. (25ml.) port

1¾ pints (1 litre) red wine

9 fl. oz. (250ml.) stock (game)

thyme, parsley and garlic

peppercorns

redcurrant jelly

butter

Make the venison sauce by roasting the venison bones in the oven. Add the mirepoix, flame with brandy and de-glaze with red wine. Add the game stock, thyme, parsley, crushed pepper, chopped garlic and bay leaf. Simmer for 1 hour. Strain and reduce by half. Add the redcurrant jelly and port and finally whisk in knobs of butter.

Season the partridges and cover the breasts with back fat. Roast in the oven keeping the meat pink. Set aside to cool. Bone out.

Chop the bones and return to the roasting tin. Add the finely chopped shallots and sweat. Deglaze the pan with the white wine, brandy and port. Add the thyme, peppercorns, bayleaf and rosemary. Bring to the boil and simmer for 5 minutes. Strain and reduce to half the quantity. Finish by whisking in knobs of butter.

Season the venison and fry in a little oil in a hot pan. Keep the flesh pink.

For the apple wedges, toss the apple in a little butter and cinnamon and sugar. Arrange the apple wedges in a flat serving dish, add a little crème fraiche and gratinate in the oven.

For the partridge:

3 partridge
pork back fat
2 shallots, finely chopped
½ pint (275ml.) white wine
1 fl. oz. (25ml.) brandy
1 fl. oz. (25ml.) port
sprigs of thyme and rosemary
10 peppercorns
½ bay leaf
butter

For the apple wedges:

apples
sugar
cinnamon
crème fraiche

For the celeriac purée:

celeriac
chicken stock
lemon juice
crème fraiche

For the celeriac purée, dice the celeriac and put into a pan. Cover with chicken stock, add a little lemon juice and a knob of butter. Simmer until soft. Liquidise the contents of the pan with a little knob of butter and crème fraiche.

To serve arrange the slices of saddle of venison, partially covered with the venison sauce and the slices of breast of partridge with port wine sauce. Garnish with apple wedges and celeriac purée.

Feuilleté of Game with Port and Rosemary

Corse Lawn House, Corse Lawn
Chef/proprietor Baba Hine

1 hare
6 pigeons
1 grouse
1 lb. (450g.) venison
8 oz. (225g.) gammon
6 leeks, chopped
1 onion, chopped
6 sticks celery, chopped
port
rosemary spikes
puff pastry cases

Remove the flesh from the game and chop into dice.

Make a rich, reduced stock with the bones.

Sauté the chopped vegetables and diced game in butter till browned. Add the stock and port in equal quantities and season to taste. Simmer for an hour. Add the rosemary.

Remove from the heat and place the mixture into individual puff pastry cases and cook in the oven.

Tourte de Gibier aux Pommes

Buckland Manor, Buckland
Chef Martyn Pearn

Serves 4

2 grouse
2 partridge
4 oz. (125g.) butter
12 oz. (350g.) puff pastry
4 Golden Delicious or Granny
   Smith, peeled and sliced

For the sauce:

3½ fl. oz. (100ml.) Madeira
18 fl. oz. (500ml.) veal stock
2 oz. (50g.) butter

In a hot oven roast the seasoned birds in the butter till pink. Remove and allow to cool. When cold remove the breasts, retaining the carcass for the sauce.

Slice each breast horizontally into three equal portions. Inlay the breasts with slices of apple and reform into oval shapes. Place each breast onto puff pastry, cover with more sliced apple and wrap in the pastry. Brush with egg wash and cook for 20 minutes in a medium oven.

To make the sauce, chop up the carcasses and place in a saucepan. Add the Madeira and veal stock, bring to the boil and skim. Reduce by half and then whisk in the butter. Strain through a fine sieve and check the seasoning.

Game Tourte with Cranberries

Hilaire, London
Chef/proprietor Simon Hopkinson

8 oz. (225g.) puff pastry
1 egg
cranberry sauce, good quality
   ready made or compôt made
   by cooking fresh cranberries
   in red wine and sugar till
   tender

For the farce:

8 oz. (225g.) game meat (hare,
   grouse, partridge etc.)
4 oz. (125g.) pork back fat, cut
   into tiny dice
4 oz. (125g.) raw duck fois gras,
   cut into tiny dice
4 oz. (125g.) chicken or duck
   liver
2 eggs
½ teaspoon quatre epices
salt and pepper to taste
3 tablespoons port or Madeira

For the farce, mince together finely the game meat and chicken and duck liver. Add all the other ingredients and place in a large roomy bowl or the bowl of a mixer. Mix together thoroughly. Leave in the fridge over night covered in cling film to allow the flavours to develop.

For the pastry, either buy some good quality puff pastry or make your own to a favourite recipe. Either way you will need about 8 oz. (225g.) and an egg for the glaze.

Roll out the pastry very thinly and cut into rounds about 5″ (12.5 cm.) across. You will need 8 circles. Lay out 4 and divide the mixture between them leaving about ¾″ (1.5cm.) gap around the edge. If you feel you have too much mixture (and it is wise not to over-fill the tourtes) then you can make extra tourtes and freeze them successfully or simply just freeze the mixture.

With the other 4 circles brush the edges with beaten egg thoroughly, and invert them over the farce and seal the edges by pinching with your fingers until they are well sealed. They should resemble round Cornish pasties.

2 small shallots, finely chopped
2 small cloves garlic, finely
chopped
½ teaspoon fresh thyme leaves

For the sauce:

carcasses from the game used,
chopped up
4 fl. oz. (125ml.) port
4 fl. oz. (125ml.) red wine
1 dessertspoon redcurrant jelly
1 teaspoon crushed
peppercorns
½ pint (275ml.) water
mirepoix of chopped
vegetables (i.e. carrot, celery,
leek, onion, garlic)
salt and pinch of ground cloves
1 teaspoon tomato purée
1 teaspoon flour
3 oz. (75g.) butter

To make the sauce, take a large roomy saucepan and melt the butter till golden brown. Throw in the carcasses and sauté until well coloured. Add the vegetables and tomato purée and carry on frying until they are well coloured. Add the port and flame. Reduce until all the liquid has disappeared. Add the flour and cook for about a further minute. Add the red wine, water, redcurrant jelly, peppercorns, some salt and the ground cloves. Simmer gently for 1 hour, skimming the sauce well. Strain through a fine sieve and adjust the seasoning if necessary.

To cook the tourte, heat your oven to 425F/220C/Gas 7. Place a flat baking sheet on the top shelf for 10 minutes (this helps cook the bottoms of the tourte well). Butter the flat baking sheet, glaze the tourte with egg and cook for 10 minutes or until well browned and glossy. Serve immediately surrounded by the sauce and garnish with the cranberries.

Cold Game Pie

Popjoys, Bath
Chef/proprietor Ali Golden

Serves 6–8

3 teal, plucked and drawn

1 small wild rabbit, skinned, cleaned and jointed

6 oz. (175g.) piece of green bacon

1 onion, sliced

2 leeks, sliced

2 carrots, sliced

1 bunch parsley stalks

pinch of mace

1 bay leaf

piece of lemon rind

4–6 peppercorns

water

2 glasses burgundy

4 oz. (125g.) mushrooms

3 hard-boiled eggs (or several quails eggs)

4 oz. (125g.) cooked tongue, thinly sliced

1 oz. (25g.) gelatine

1½ lb. (700g.) shortcrust pastry

Put the game meat in a casserole dish with the bacon, onion, leeks, carrots, parsley, mace, bay leaf, lemon rind, peppercorns and water to cover. Bring to the boil, lower the heat, skim the surface and simmer for 30–40 minutes until the meat is tender.

Whilst the meat is cooking prepare the forcemeat balls. Fry the onion in butter until golden and then mix it with the breadcrumbs and sage and bind the mixture with a bit of egg (lightly beaten). Shape the mixture into small balls and shallow fry in oil. Drain on kitchen paper and set aside. Fry the mushrooms gently for a couple of minutes. Drain and reserve.

Remove the cooked meat from the stock, including the bacon, and leave to cool. Cut the meat from the bones and chop into 1″ (2.5cm.) pieces, keeping the different meats separate.

Return the bones from the game meat to the stock pan and simmer for at least an hour until you have a strong reduced stock, about 1 pint (570ml.). Add the burgundy to the stock and season to taste.

Grease a collapsible pie or cake tin with a removable bottom. Roll out the pastry to about ½″ (1cm.) thick and line the tin with two-thirds of it.

Arrange a layer of cooked teal and then stuffing balls in the tin. Scatter the bacon and mushrooms on top and arrange the boiled eggs on top of this. Cover this with a layer of tongue and then finish with a layer of rabbit. Pour in the stock until it comes half way up the pie dish. Cover with a lid of pastry and decorate with trimmings. Make a hole for the steam to escape.

Brush the pastry with egg and bake the pie for 20–30 minutes or until golden brown at 425F/220C/gas 7. Leave to cool.

Melt the appropriate amount of gelatine in the remaining stock reduction and then carefully pour into the pie through the central hole until almost to the top. Allow to set overnight before turning out.

Thornbury Game Pie

Thornbury Castle, Thornbury
Chef Colin Hingston

2 lbs. (900g.) diced game meat
  – venison, pheasant,
  partridge, grouse, wild duck,
  hare etc, as available
olive oil
2 oz. (50g.) chopped celery
2 oz. (50g.) chopped carrot
2 oz. (50g.) chopped fennel
4 oz. (125g.) chopped onion
1 clove garlic, crushed
1 pinch sage
2 pinches of thyme
2 tablespoons of tomato
  purée
2 large glasses of port
1 large glass of red wine
strong brown veal stock
2 tablespoons of redcurrant
  jelly
salt and pepper

Heat the oil in a frying pan until smoking. Put in some of the meat and stir until well browned. Tip the meat into a saucepan and repeat until all the meat is brown. Repeat this same process with the vegetables, adding some tomato purée to each batch.

When all the meat and vegetables are fried, de-glaze the frying pan with the port and add this to the saucepan. Add the garlic, herbs and seasoning along with the red wine and redcurrant jelly to the meat. Just cover the meat with the veal stock and simmer gently for 1½–2 hours until tender. Add more stock if necessary. Cool.

Put into a pie dish and cover with puff pastry and bake slowly until brown.

Notes

Notes

Notes

Drybridge

Peat Inn

Gullane

Ullswater

Windermere

Pool in Wharfdale

Kenilworth

Bakewell

Dublin

Llandudno

Loughborough

Gorey

Oundle

Shanagarry

Buckland

Bishops Tachbrook

Diss

Horton

Corse Lawn

Malvern Wells

Stratford-on-Avon

Ledbury

Llandewi Skirrid

Wye

Bicester

Colchester

Cheltenham

London

Bath

Bristol

East Grinstead

Oakhill

Canterbury

Ston Easton

Haslemere

Folkestone

Williton

Pulborough

Ashburton

Romsey

Lewes

Tunbridge Wells

Chagford

Botallack

Shepton Mallet

Hinton Charterhouse

Dartmouth

Gulworthy

Jersey

124

Restaurant Addresses

Billesley Manor	– Billesley, Nr. Stratford-upon-Avon.	0789 763737
Bodysgallen Hall	– Llandudno, Gwynedd.	0492 84466
Restaurant Bosquet	– 97a Warwick Road, Kenilworth.	0926 52463
Bowlish House	– Shepton Mallet, Somerset.	0749 2022
Buckland Manor	– Buckland, Gloucestershire.	0386 852626
Carved Angel	– 2 South Embankment, Dartmouth.	08043 2465
La Ciboulette	– 24–26 Suffolk Road, Cheltenham.	0242 573449
Le Coq Hardi	– 35 Pembroke Road, Dublin.	Dublin 689070
Corse Lawn House	– Corse Lawn, Gloucestershire.	045278 479
Count House	– Botallack, Penzance.	0736 788588
Country Garden	– 22 East Street, Ashburton, Devon.	0364 53431
Croque-en-Bouche	– 221 Wells Road, Malvern Wells.	06845 65612
L'Escargot	– 48 Greek Street, London W1.	01 437 2679
Fischer's	– Woodhouse, Bath Street, Bakewell.	062 981 2687
Flowers	– 27 Monmouth Street, Bath.	0225 313774
Fox & Goose	– Fressingfield, Diss, Norfolk.	037986 247
French Partridge	– Horton, Nr. Northampton.	0604 870033
Gidleigh Park	– Chagford, Devon.	064 73 2367
Gravetye Manor	– Sharpthorne, Nr. East Grinstead.	0342 810567
Hilaire	– 68 Old Brompton Road, London.	01 584 8993
Homewood Park	– Hinton Charterhouse, Bath.	022 122 2643
Hope End	– Ledbury, Hereford & Worcester.	0531 3613
Kenwards	– 151a High Street, Lewes, Sussex.	0273 472343
Longueville Manor	– Jersey, Channel Islands.	0534 25501
Mallory Court	– Bishops Tachbrook, Nr. Leamington Spa.	0926 30214
Marlfield House	– Gorey, Co. Wexford.	Gorey 21124
Michael's	– 129 Hotwell Road, Bristol.	0272 276190
Morels	– 25 Lower Street, Haslemere, Surrey.	0428 51462
Old Manor House	– 21 Palmerston Street, Romsey.	0794 517353
Old Monastery	– Drybridge, Banffshire.	0542 32660

Ortolan	–	Old Vicarage, Shinfield, Berkshire.	0734 883783
Partners 23	–	23 Stonecot Hill, Sutton.	01 644 7743
Paul's	–	2a Bouverie Road West, Folkestone.	0303 59697
The Peat Inn	–	Peat Inn, Fife.	033 484 206
Pomegranates	–	94 Grosvenor Road, London SW1.	01 828 6560
Pool Court	–	Pool in Wharfedale, West Yorkshire.	0532 842288
Popjoys	–	Sawclose, Bath.	0225 60494
Le Poulbot	–	45 Cheapside, London EC2.	01 236 4379
Priory Hotel	–	Weston Road, Bath.	0225 331922
Restaurant Roger Burdell	–	Manor House, Loughborough.	0509 231813
Roger's	–	4 High Street, Windermere, Cumbria.	096 62 4954
Royal Crescent Hotel	–	Royal Crescent, Bath.	0225 319090
Restaurant Seventy-Four	–	74 Wincheap, Canterbury.	0227 67411
Sharrow Bay	–	Honiton Road, Ullswater, Cumbria.	085 36 301
Stane Street Hollow	–	Pulborough, West Sussex.	07982 2819
Ston Easton Park	–	Ston Easton, Somerset.	076121 631
Thackeray's House	–	85 London Road, Tunbridge Wells.	0892 37558
Thornbury Castle	–	Thornbury, Nr. Bristol.	0454 412647
Tyrrells	–	6 & 8 New Street, Oundle.	08322 2347
Walnut Tree Inn	–	Llandewi Skirrid, Gwent.	0873 2797
Wife of Bath	–	4 Upper Bridge Street, Wye.	0233 812540
Woods	–	9–13 Alfred Street, Bath.	0225 314812
Woods	–	Bignell View, Bicester.	08692 41444

Index